# LEEDS

## THEN AND NOW

First published in the United Kingdom in 2019 by
PAVILION BOOKS
an imprint of Pavilion Books Company Ltd.
43 Great Ormond Street, London WC1N 3HZ

"Then and Now" is a registered trademark of Salamander Books Limited,
a division of Pavilion Books Group.

© 2019 Salamander Books Limited, a division of Pavilion Books Group.

ISBN-13: 978-1-911595-91-5

Printed in China

10 9 8 7 6 5 4 3 2 1

## PICTURE CREDITS

The majority of the "Then" photographs come from the Leodis archive managed by Leeds
Library & Information Service. Others were supplied by the Thoresby Society, pages 10, 14, 18,
20, 26, 32, 38, 42, 44, 56, 80, 82, 98, 102, 104, 106, 114, 116, 130, 132, 136, 138, 160; the Pavilion Image
Library, pages 12, 24, 84, 88, 94, 108, 124, 128; Mirrorpix, page 34; Ken Gibson, page 54; Alamy,
page 90.

The "Now" photographs were taken by David Major with the exception of pages 9 and 41, Eric
Musgrave; pages 25 and 91 Alamy.

## DEDICATION

This book is dedicated to my paternal grandparents, Arthur and Bertha Musgrave, of East
End Park, Leeds.

## AUTHOR'S NOTE AND ACKNOWLEDGEMENTS

In contrast to similar photographic books on Leeds, I have chosen to concentrate tightly
on the centre of the city, with a bias towards its retail and commercial locations, so here
there is no Kirkstall Abbey nor Temple Newsam, no Elland Road nor Headingley. As well
as being major employers of Leeds folk, the city's shops and stores touch everyone's lives
and residents of every suburb know the city centre even if they are unfamiliar with other
residential districts.

I must thank my dear friend and Leeds lass Beverley Cluderay Forrest for her constant
encouragement, guidance and enthusiasm for the project. Sally Hughes of the Local and
Family History Department of Leeds Central Library was a brilliant and reliable source of
images and information, assisted in the later stages of the process by her colleague Karen
Marr. Patrick Gillett, honorary librarian of The Thoresby Society, was generous in his help
and allowing me access to the Leeds historical society's photographic archive. The staff of
the Leeds Library were kind to scan the images I had chosen. Edward Ziff, chairman and
chief executive of Town Centre Securities, kindly shared with me his amazing knowledge of
the property scene in Leeds.

I also wish to thank the many Leodensians who helped identify obscure buildings when
I posted images on Facebook. David Major, the photographer of the "Now" images, did an
excellent job even though we were communicating remotely and never met.

## BIBLIOGRAPHY

The remarkable online archive, *www.leodis.net*, managed by Leeds Library & Information
Service, was my essential research resource for this book. My main printed reference
work was the exhaustive *Pevsner Architectural Guides: Leeds*, by Susan Wrathmell (Yale
University Press, 2008).
Among the many other books I looked at, these were the most helpful:
*Around Leeds: A City Centre Reinvented*, by John Stillwell and Rachael Unsworth (Leeds
University Press, 2008)
*Images of Leeds 1850-1960*, by Peter Brears (Breedon Books, 1992)
*Leeds*, by Ivan Broadhead (Smith Settle, 1990)
*Leeds Then and Now*, by Brian Godward (Leeds Civic Trust, 1999)
*Portrait of Leeds*, by Brian Thompson (Robert Hale, 1971)
*The Merrion Centre: The First Fifty Years* (Town Centre Securities, 2014)

# LEEDS
## THEN AND NOW

ERIC MUSGRAVE

NOW PHOTOGRAPHY
DAVID MAJOR

PAVILION

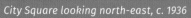

*City Square looking north-east, c. 1936*     p. 10

*Park Place, c. 1972*     p. 20

*The Town Hall, c. 1905*     p. 26

*Leeds University, 1945*     p. 30

*The Merrion Centre, 1964*     p. 34

*Park Row, 1944*     p. 44

*Schofields, 1949*     p. 50

*Thornton's Arcade, 1956*     p. 58

*Lewis's Department Store, 1932*     p. 66

*Odeon Cinema, 1949* p. 68

*Eastgate Roundabout, 1967* p. 76

*Leeds City Markets, c. 1910* p. 90

*Third White Cloth Hall, 1906* p. 98

*Briggate looking north from Boar Lane, c. 1933* p. 114

*Kardomah Café, c. 1936* p. 122

*Queens Arcade from Briggate, c. 1900* p. 124

*Looking eastwards from Leeds Bridge, c. 1910* p. 136

*Temple Works, c. 1935* p. 142

# LEEDS

## THEN AND NOW INTRODUCTION

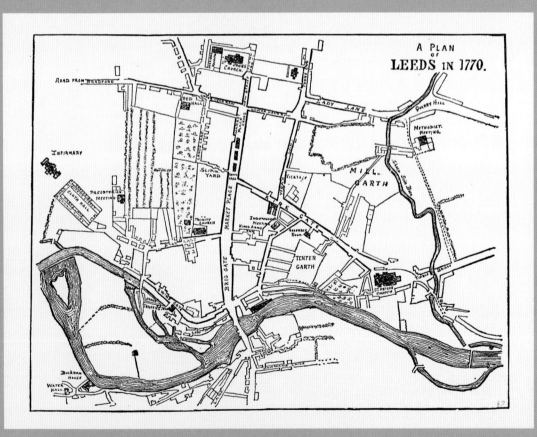

Received wisdom states that Leeds is a product of the Industrial Revolution, a great Victorian northern industrial city shaped by the manufacturing boom that began in the late 18th century and employed thousands of people for almost 200 years in industries like textiles, clothing manufacture, metalworking and engineering.

The suburbs of modern Leeds include the ruins of the twelfth-century Cistercian monastery at Kirkstall and its ecclesiastical contemporary, the Norman church of St John at Adel, but the centre of the city is distinctly lacking in ancient monuments considering that the metropolis is the fourth most populous in the UK with more than 760,000 residents in 2016.

Inarguably, the best-known and most memorable buildings in Leeds were indeed built in Queen Victoria's reign, or conceived during it and completed soon after Edward VII succeeded her in 1901. The rebuilt parish church of St Peter was consecrated in 1842. The Town Hall was completed in 1858. The Corn Exchange was opened in 1863. The iconic City Square was laid out between 1893 and 1903 after Leeds was granted city status. The flamboyant shopping arcades off Briggate were erected between 1898 and 1904. The City Market building on Kirkgate was opened in 1904.

So, on the face of it, the received wisdom holds good, but contemporary visitors to Leeds enjoying the bustling concentration of shopping streets and many restaurants and bars are probably unaware that the layout of the city was defined long before the Industrial Revolution powered into life and the Empress of India acceded to the throne in 1837.

Contrary to what might be expected or found in other cities, neither City Square nor the Town Hall is the focus of

Leeds. The centre of Leeds is the wide thoroughfare of Briggate and it has been since at least 1207 when the path northwards from the crossing over the River Aire – literally the bridge gate – was established. As with most settlements, what was to become Leeds started out as dwellings next to the water. The first mention of Leeds was made by the scholarly monk The Venerable Bede in his *Ecclesiastical History of the English People* of 731 AD, when he referred to the region of Loidis, but he was scant on details.

The Domesday Book of 1086 gathered more information on the district, listing in addition to 'Ledes' itself settlements now known as the suburbs of Armley, Beeston, Bramley, Chapel Allerton, Headingley, Hunslet, Coldcotes and Osmondthorpe. In 1086, Leeds became part of the huge tracts awarded to Norman nobleman Ilbert de Lacy. Drinkers in The Scarborough Arms, the historic pub on Bishopgate Street across from the modern railway station, are downing pints on the presumed site of the medieval manorial hall.

In 1207, lord of the manor Maurice Paynel granted a charter to the burgesses of Leeds, which led to the laying out of Briggate and the burgages, or narrow plots of leased land, that ran at right angles to it. These in time became enclosed yards that were succeeded in the late nineteenth century by shopping arcades like Thornton's and Queen's. Briggate pubs like Whitelock's and The Ship are in ginnels that were burgages hundreds of years ago, and Harvey Nichols, the Yorkshire outpost of the *Absolutely Fabulous* department store group that opened in 1996 as a glossy symbol of revitalised Leeds, sits over one.

Charles I granted the city its first charter in 1626. The owls on Leeds' coat of arms were borrowed from the family crest of its first alderman of the period, Sir John Savile. So, the modern Leeds boasts a deeply layered history that might not be obvious at first. It also has a long track record in going for something new, of making a bold development. An early example was Wilson's Park Estate of the late 1700s, a residential enclave to take the wealthy classes westwards away from the overcrowded areas around Briggate and Kirkgate. Much of the estate is well preserved as the Georgian Leeds district to the south of the Town Hall. Another bold masterplan resulted in the creation of The Headrow in the late 1920s and early 1930s. All the old buildings on the north side (and a few on the south) were pulled down to realise Sir Reginald Blomfield's unified vision for the northern edge of the shopping district.

The vast Quarry Hill Flats development of the late 1930s, although it survived only 40 years, was another piece of Leeds building bravado. Less visually arresting, but again showing the city's propensity to embrace the new, the Inner Ring Road, constructed a short distance to the north of The Headrow from the early 1960s, was a significant engineering feat. With the M1 reaching the city from the south in 1972, Leeds proudly described itself as 'the motorway city of the seventies'.

Ironically the 1970s and early 1980s saw Leeds take a significant dip in prosperity as its traditional manufacturing industries disappeared, but since the mid 1980s a series of large-scale initiatives has picked the city up, dusted it off and produced a revitalised sense of civic pride. At the forefront of this remarkable late twentieth-century renaissance was the transformation of the near-derelict waterfront of the River Aire and the hugely successful refurbishment of Frank Matcham's glorious arcades as the Victoria Quarter. The 2016 opening of the Victoria Gate shopping centre on a long-derelict patch of land next to the market only added to Leeds' long-standing reputation as a retailing hotspot.

In contrast to the positives, one worry for any lover of Leeds is how some of its oldest buildings are seeking a relevant modern role. Its trio of historic city centre churches – St John the Evangelist (1634), Holy Trinity (1727) and St Peter, now Leeds Minster (1842) – are among the oldest buildings, but the least visited, at least by active worshippers. As monuments, however, they are safe for future generations, but the same cannot be said for the unique Temple Works in Holbeck. John Marshall's vast flax mill of 1840, with its remarkable frontage modelled on an Egyptian temple, really does fit into the received wisdom of Leeds having boomed thanks to the Industrial Revolution. Yet, structurally compromised, it has been on Historic England's 'At Risk' list for decades. Help appears to be at hand, with the council actively supporting a sympathetic developer. Rescuing Temple Works is a massive and expensive challenge, but a successful outcome here would be typical of Leeds, which has a great tradition for preserving and updating Then for Now.

1897

# CITY SQUARE

Leeds' central plaza, created to mark its status as a city in 1893

8

LEFT: City Square rivals the Town Hall as the quintessential symbol of Leeds. By far the largest open space in the city centre, it was conceived and constructed between 1893 and 1903 to celebrate Leeds being granted city status by Queen Victoria in 1893. The idea of Lord Mayor and industrialist T. Walter Harding, it was designed by William Bakewell. In this image from April 14th 1897, advertising hoardings surround the construction site. Part of the square had been covered by the Coloured or Mixed Cloth Hall, built in 1757 and the largest building of Georgian Leeds. Almost 400 feet long and 200 feet wide, it had wings that could accommodate nearly 2,000 stalls of textile sellers and a central courtyard into which 20,000 people could fit. It was demolished in 1890. At the south side is the original Queens Hotel, designed by William Belton Perkin for Midland Railway. It was opened in 1863 and extended in 1867 and 1898.

ABOVE: Ostensibly the 'centre' of Leeds, in reality City Square is set slightly to the west of the busy shopping district, but it is still the first part of the city seen by travellers leaving Leeds railway station. Reconfigured several times since 1903 to suit the demands of modern urban traffic, it remains an emotional location for sons and daughters of Leeds. The buildings on its circumference have been changed regularly over the decades – and increased in height – and their purpose has been developed too. The Queens, although in a much grander form, is still a hotel in front of the station, but beyond it are some of the new buildings that epitomise Leeds' economic and commercial revival and resurgence since the mid 1980s.

# CITY SQUARE LOOKING NORTH-EAST

The offices of financial and legal firms keep rising taller

LEFT: In this image from the 1930s, the huge bronze equestrian statue of Edward the Black Prince (1330–1376) is on its original circular raised platform about 100 feet in diameter, surrounded by a balustrade of polished marble. Designed by Thomas Brock, who had designed the statue of Prince Albert for the Albert Memorial in London, the statue was cast in Belgium. It took seven years to make and was brought in pieces by barge via Hull on the Aire & Calder Navigation, the waterway that linked Leeds to the sea from 1700. The son of Edward III had no obvious connection to Leeds, but he was viewed by T. Walter Harding, however, as a suitably heroic national figure to grace the new plaza. The statue was unveiled to thousands of spectators at noon on Wednesday, September 16th, 1903, but the choice of the hero of the Battle of Crecy was a controversial one.

ABOVE: Old and new Leeds are contrasting neighbours on City Square. At left, the 1896 Post Office is dwarfed by Number 1 City Square, opened in 1996. Designed by Abbey Holford Rowe, its glazed atrium and lift shaft made this 12-storey structure a striking addition to the skyline. Commissioned by Norwich Union, it replaced the previous Leeds base of the financial services company, which stood from 1967 until 1995 on the site of the 1901 Standard Life Assurance building, seen in the image opposite. The pale-coloured building at the centre is the 10-storey Number 1 Park Row, by architects Fletcher Joseph, opened in 1998. Its dome is meant, perhaps, to echo the decorative Edwardian style of a century earlier. Priestley Hall, previously on the site, came down in 1968. Behind Mill Hill Chapel is the City Exchange office block, which is part of the Trinity Shopping Centre on Albion Street. The Park Plaza hotel is at the extreme right.

c. 1928

# THE GENERAL POST OFFICE

The mail-sorting building that became luxurious apartments

LEFT: The finest building constructed as part of the City Square development of 1893–1903, the splendid General Post Office was designed by Henry Tanner, a prominent London-based architect who had been a surveyor in Leeds in the early 1880s. Displaying Tanner's version of a Northern Renaissance style, it was opened in 1896 and occupied part of the site of the Georgian-era Coloured or Mixed Cloth Hall, which stood here from 1757 to 1890. The Post Office cost £75,000 (around £9.5 million in today's values) to build and its clock tower became something of a Leeds landmark. This building replaced a previous post office that was sited just to the north.

ABOVE: A Grade II-listed building since 1974, the former General Post Office ceased to provide Royal Mail services in 2004. In 2006 it was restored, the ground floor becoming a bar-restaurant and two of the upper floors being converted into apartments. Known initially as Residence 6 and later Quebecs Luxury Apartments, they comprise yet more City Square accommodation alongside The Queens and the Park Plaza. The restoration has allowed a new generation to admire the building's ashlar, or finely dressed stonework, and its many adornments, such as statues of Art and Science, which are coated with green moss. A rear part of the large building comprises the City Campus for Leeds Beckett University. Included in this is Cloth Hall Court, which is operated as a conference centre.

# PARK PLAZA HOTEL

The former office block was Leeds' tallest building when opened in 1966

BELOW: This 1967 image shows City Square soon after it had been "reduced and severely altered", as Susan Wrathmell writes in the 2005 version of the *Pevsner Architectural Guide* for Leeds. The Black Prince's raised platform is gone. The skyline is dominated by the unlovely Exchange House, opened in 1965 on the site of the Royal Exchange House office building, whose Gothic spire and clock tower are to be seen on page 10. The tower is one of the tallest buildings in Leeds, reaching up 225 feet.

It dwarfs the neighbouring soot-black Mill Hill Utilitarian Chapel, opened on December 27th, 1848, and the only building on City Square predating the square's construction from 1893. To the left of the chapel at the end of Park Row is Priestley Hall from 1858, named after Joseph Priestley, the eminent chemist, who was born in Birstall, just outside Leeds. He was minister of Mill Hill Chapel from 1763 to 1773.

1967

BELOW: In 2002 City Square was remodelled under the guidance of Leeds Civic Architect John Thorp, who changed it from having an island at its centre. The pavement now continues in front of the old General Post Office so traffic exits north-westwards via Quebec Street instead of racing behind the Black Prince. Additional lighting, animated water jets and planting were installed, but as the trees mature the splendour of the original open space has been diluted. The equestrian statue of Edward III's son does not dominate the space as it once did. In contrast to the large-scale developments that Leeds enjoyed in the Victorian era, the hotchpotch of styles from the 1960s onwards seen here do not make for a cohesive or attractive panorama. Typical of the abrasive architectural styles added in recent years is the domed brick building right behind the old Yorkshire Bank, which is part of a new development just off Bishopgate Street.

1949

# AIRE STREET

Creative agencies have replaced manufacturing workshops just off City Square

LEFT: Leeds prided itself on the variety of its commercial activities, which embraced manufacturing and wholesaling, importing and exporting. In this 1949 photograph of Aire Street, which runs south-west from City Square and the railway station, the premises include those of T. B. Morley (electrical and sanitary showrooms), J. P. McDougall (decorators' merchants), S. Grant (paper factory) and Hector Gollan & Son (wholesale jewellers). The street is named after the river on which Leeds stands. The Aire rises in Malham Tarn in the Yorkshire Dales and flows into the River Ouse near Goole. A settlement that became Leeds was built on a crossing place formed by the silt dropped by two tributaries of the Aire: the Meanwood Beck from the north and the Hol Beck from the south. Part of the Aire below Leeds, known as the Aire & Calder Navigation, was converted into a canal from 1700. The River Aire is an evocative reference for any native of Leeds.

ABOVE: Like most of central Leeds bordering the river, Aire Street has been improved as part of the refurbishment of the waterfront since the mid 1980s. A good number of its Victorian properties are still in use, but the tenants are likely to be from creative industries like graphic design rather than engineering manufacturers or wholesalers. Just seen on the left are the first floors of the 11-storey Princes Exchange office block, opened in 2000. The huge mural was commissioned by Japanese entertainment company Konami for the release of its game *Metal Gear Rising: Revengeance* in February 2013. East London-based contemporary art specialists EndOfTheLine's representation of the game's protagonist Raiden appeared only in Leeds, Liverpool and London. At the end of the street is Central Square, built on the long-derelict site of the Leeds Central railway station. Designed by DLA Architecture and opened in 2016, the building has won awards for its energy efficiency.

# EAST PARADE

Laid out during the building boom in Georgian Leeds

BELOW: East Parade was laid out between 1779 and 1789 as part of Wilson's Park Estate, which offered a higher class of residential housing, slightly to the west of the crowded town centre. However, the oldest buildings in this 1940 image are from the nineteenth century. Looking north from the junction with St Paul's Street, at the top we see the imposing edifice of Central Library, one of the municipal buildings built in 1878–84 by George Corson, one of Leeds' prominent architects. The large light-coloured building is the Pearl Assurance building. Its neighbours on the east side include the Alliance Assurance and the Guardian Assurance offices – this is the heart of Leeds' financial and legal district. On the west side, commercial concerns range from Holt & Co. "Wholesale Warehousemen" to J. G. Porter, a dealer in typewriters and stationery, and a supplier of insulated electric cables. The policeman wears large white gauntlets as he is on point duty.

BELOW: Like Park Row, its slightly grander neighbour to the east, East Parade has seen some of its buildings upgraded and retain their use as commercial offices. Others have kept their Victorian extravagance but have seen a marked change in use. Finance and insurance have often been replaced by food and drink. Eagle Star and later Zurich Insurance have been tenants of 1 East Parade, the red office block here on the corner of St Paul's Street. Built in 1992–1994 by William Gower and Partners, its modern style is meant to echo the stripy design beloved by Victorian architect Alfred Waterhouse. Facing it at No. 29 is what is now called Minerva. The 11-storey office block was built in 1966 and has been refurbished inside and out several times since. It has housed offices for Guardian Assurance and Royal Bank of Scotland and has tenants from similar sectors today. A bar-restaurant occupies part of the ground floor.

c. 1972

# PARK PLACE

A parade of Georgian houses originally with views over fields to the River Aire

ABOVE: The LS1 postcode district covers the heart of "professional" Leeds, the traditional home of its financial services, property and legal fraternity. Park Place was constructed during the 1770s as part of the Wilson's Park Estate. In those days it afforded views across fields to the river. This image shows the south-facing side of the street. Seen in the centre with a gabled front, No. 6 had been home to Reverend Dr. Walter Hook during his time as vicar of Leeds (1837–1859) and was subsequently used as the vicarage for the parish church, which he was instrumental in remodelling. Hook had moved here from the previous manse in Vicar Lane to allow a covered market to be built on Kirkgate. In this 1970s photograph, the building is occupied by British Relay, which supplied wired television services across the UK.

ABOVE: The compact enclave of Georgian Leeds around Park Place is a conservation area and most, if not all, of the buildings on this side of the street have been Grade II listed since 1963. The detailed descriptions of each address on the Historic England website reveal the nineteenth- and twentieth-century alterations made to these once-residential properties, but there is a remarkable number that are virtually unchanged externally. As expected in this corner of the city, the tenants today are mainly from the professions, such as law firms, financial service companies, estate agencies, chartered surveyors and accountants. Private health clinics, a language school and a printer – which is presumably kept busy by its neighbours' requirements – are exceptions. Much of Reverend Hook's residence at No. 6 is occupied by a recruitment company. At the west end of the street is an office block called 21 Queen Street. Its fourth and fifth floors were added as part of a refurbishment in 2015.

c. 1961

# ST PAUL'S HOUSE
The amazing Hispano-Moorish warehouse built for clothing magnate John Barran

LEFT: John Barran was instrumental in shaping Leeds' reputation as the world's capital for mass production of ready-to-wear tailored clothing. Having moved to Leeds from London in 1842 to open a tailoring shop, in the 1850s Barran was an early adopter of the industrial sewing machines developed by the American Isaac Singer. In 1858 he developed a band knife that enabled many layers of suiting cloth to be cut at once, so speeding up the manufacturing process. The lasting symbol of the strength of his business is this fantastic Hispano-Moorish building, opened in 1878 as a factory and warehouse. The 164-foot-long structure in red and pink brick with terracotta, at the western end of St Paul's Street, was designed by the Leeds-based architect Thomas Ambler, to whom Barran was a patron and friend. Barran was Lord Mayor of Leeds in 1870–71 and a Liberal MP for the city from 1876 to 1885.

BELOW: A side view of the magnificent St Paul's House photographed from across Park Square.

c. 1961

RIGHT: John Barran had his main factory at nearby Chorley Lane and in 1904 the Public Benefit Footwear Company, a national chain, took over the building. Neglected over the years, the property was scheduled for demolition in the early 1970s, but fortunately was reprieved. It was completely gutted and only the facades of Barran's extraordinary Moorish-style warehouse were retained. Much of the parapet and minaret decoration, which had been in terracotta, was duplicated in glass fibre. Converted to offices, it had its entrance moved from the corner of 20–22 St Paul's Street to 23 Park Square. The remodelling earned the building a Leeds Civic Trust award in 1979. Befitting its location in Leeds' legal district, law firms are among its tenants. St Paul's House, as the building is now known, has been Grade II listed since 1963.

c. 1968

# PARK SQUARE

A rare, quiet open space in Leeds city centre, in the professionals' district

LEFT: The north side of Park Square was built between 1793 and 1815, with the square itself having been laid out in 1788. The houses of Park Place were thought at the time to be superior, even though each house here was built to the owner's distinct specifications. Originally constructed as private homes for the well-to-do who wished to be somewhat removed from the busy town centre slightly to the east, Park Square buildings were extensively converted to warehouses and offices in the nineteenth century, with legal firms being very common residents. Within the square stood the 1894 bronze statue of the Greek sorceress Circe by Alfred Drury, who sculpted the eight similar forms, representing Morn and Even, for Leeds City Square. The proximity of Park Square to the seat of civic power, the Town Hall, is clearly seen in this image.

ABOVE: The merchants, clergy, lawyers and surgeons who were the principal residents of Park Square when it was created in the late eighteenth and early nineteenth centuries have long since relocated. A link with those days is provided, however, by the many law firms, barristers' chambers and several private health clinics that occupy the properties today. All the Georgian buildings are Grade II listed. The square was well-known to generations of Leeds citizens because No. 11, on the east side, once the home of engineer and Leeds mayor Peter Fairbairn, was for many years Leeds Register Office. Today, the square is one of only six public spaces in the city centre maintained by Leeds City Council (the others are Woodhouse, Hanover, Queen and Millennium squares, plus Merrion Street Gardens). Today, to see *Circe*, visitors must walk the short distance to the Art Gallery, to where the badly weathered statue was moved in 2008 for restoration and preservation.

1905

# THE TOWN HALL
The stupendous symbol of Leeds' civic pride, designed by the previously unknown Cuthbert Brodrick

LEFT: The majestic Town Hall came into being thanks to the Leeds Improvement Society, formed by leading citizens in 1851. In that year, John Blayds, a wealthy merchant, acquired the site for £9,500 (equivalent to £1.25 million today). In 1852 the competition to design the civic palace was won by Cuthbert Brodrick, a virtually unknown architect who had trained in Hull. The vision of the Leeds worthies was for a single building to house a concert hall for 8,000 people standing, dining rooms and kitchens, servants' halls, a council chamber, council offices and a suite for the mayor, four courtrooms and accommodation for the police. A manifestation of the wealth of Leeds, the sandstone building, which draws inspiration from French neoclassical and Baroque styles, was opened by Queen Victoria on September 7th, 1858. Its clock tower, added to his original design by Brodrick in 1856 as an afterthought, is 225 feet high, ensuring it can be spotted from many parts of the city.

ABOVE: The Town Hall looks unchanged since 1858, but there have been periodic alterations. The four white limestone lions, carved by William Day Keyworth, were not added until 1867. A memorial to Queen Victoria, unveiled on November 27th, 1905, stood outside, until it was relocated to Woodhouse Moor in 1937. In spring 1972 the building underwent its first serious cleaning, previously having been only hosed down by the fire brigade. Leeds Civic Trust, formed in 1965 to encourage high standards of architecture, opposed this, arguing the sooty hue "should stand as a symbol of the city's industrial past and as a reminder to future generations of the air pollution which the city is so successfully combatting." Grade I listed since 1951, the Town Hall lost many of its council functions to the nearby Civic Hall, opened in 1933, while its last courtroom closed in 1992. For 108 years, until 1966, the Town Hall was the tallest building in Leeds. At the time of going to press, it is the 13th tallest.

1929

# SCHOOL OF MEDICINE
Leeds had one of the first provincial medical training establishments in the UK

ABOVE: Founded in 1831 by a group of doctors and surgeons, Leeds School of Medicine was one of the first provincial centres of learning for medics in England. Its earliest schools were in East Parade and Park Street. In 1884 the school amalgamated with the Yorkshire College of Science to form a precursor of Leeds University. The School of Medicine building in Thoresby Place, seen here in 1929, was opened in 1894 alongside Leeds General Infirmary, which had been constructed between 1863 and 1868. The school, built in a Tudor Gothic style from local brick and Mansfield stone dressings, was designed by W. H. Thorp, who was also responsible for the Leeds Art Gallery a few years earlier. The entrance hall, decorated with green faience tiles made by the local Burmantofts Pottery, bears a Latin inscription from Matthew 10.8, which translates as: 'Heal the sick, cleanse the lepers; freely you have received, freely give.' The school opened with just eighty students.

ABOVE: Now known as The Old Medical School, it is still part of the Leeds teaching hospital network, offering more than a dozen undergraduate courses. A largely brick extension was added to its west side in the 1930s to a design by John C. Proctor, who was also responsible for the Algernon Firth Institute of Pathology, a delightful 1930s building right across George's Road to the west of the school's island site. During a major refurbishment in 1984–85 an upper floor was added to the old school, again mainly of brick. Having been overshadowed by George Gilbert Scott's Leeds General Infirmary building immediately to the east, the old school is now dwarfed by the Clarendon and Jubilee Wings of the Leeds General behind it, which were built in the 1980s and 1990s. Since 1974, the school has been Grade II* listed, indicating it is, in the opinion of Historic England, 'particularly important, of more than special interest'. The school boasts more than 12,600 alumni.

1945

# LEEDS UNIVERSITY

The Parkinson Building is not the oldest university building in Leeds, but it is the most famous

LEFT: In 1926, Leeds University held a competition for architects to propose a new phase of development for what was then only a small educational institution. The winners, London-based Lanchester, Lucas & Lodge, suggested a grand clock tower on the curve of Woodhouse Lane. It was not until 1936, however, when Frank Parkinson – a son of Guiseley who made his fortune from the Crompton Parkinson electrical manufacturing company – pledged £200,000 for a considerable arts and administration block, that the project could move forward. The Parkinson Building, designed in a Greek Revival style by H. V. Lanchester using Portland Stone, has become a symbol of Leeds University's post-war ambitions. Although there are lovely older buildings from the university's Victorian era behind it, it is the Parkinson that has become an emblem for the city. Seen here during construction in 1945 – it was used as a Ministry of Food store during the war – the building was formally opened in 1951.

ABOVE: In 1939, Leeds University had 1,750 full-time students. Today it has more than 31,000 and in 2019 stood at No. 10 in *The Guardian Guide to British Universities* and at No. 93 in the *QS World University Rankings*. The distinctive clock tower was designed by Thomas Lodge, H. V. Lanchester's partner in the architectural practice. The building, along with the neighbouring Brotherton Library and the chemistry and engineering block, has been Grade II listed since 1988. The campus has been extended several times since 1951, with significant additions such as the Michael Sadler Building for Arts and various engineering schools. Added nearby in 1955 was the University House refectory, a building known to rock fans across the world as the venue for The Who's *Live at Leeds* album, recorded on February 14th, 1970 and released in May that year.

# COOKRIDGE STREET / WOODHOUSE LANE

Formerly Kitson College, Leeds City College is a symbol of Leeds' importance as a centre of education

c. 1955

LEFT: Taken in the early-to-mid 1950s this photograph shows, in the centre, Cookridge Street running down a slope towards the Civic Hall and the Town Hall. To the left, Woodhouse Lane stretches down to The Headrow, while to the right it leads up to the university. The large building in the distance is the City of Leeds School; the high balcony around its rooftop playground can be made out. The large building on the corner is a Home Guard social club. Next to it on Cookridge Street is a recruiting office for the Royal Air Force. There were plenty of residential streets in the area, which explains why a large menswear establishment like Weavers could thrive here, somewhat removed from the main shopping district. The running costs of a shop here would have been much lower than in the city centre.

BELOW: Further and higher education has long been associated with Leeds. The nearby Mechanics' Institute in Cookridge Street opened in 1868 to educate working men in technical subjects. The adjacent five-storey Leeds Arts University (formerly Leeds College of Art and Design), built by Bedford & Kitson in 1903, is almost totally hidden here behind the white building, which is the Technology Campus of Leeds City College, the largest further education establishment in the city, with about 26,000 students. The building was opened in three stages between 1956 and 1960 as part of the Leeds College of Technology. Initially called the Branch College of Engineering and Science, it was renamed Kitson College in 1967 in honour of Leeds engineer and politician James Kitson. In 2009, Leeds College of Technology merged with Leeds Thomas Danby and the Park Lane College to form the new Leeds City College, and the building was rebranded.

1964

# THE MERRION CENTRE

The futuristic moving walkways proved to have a pretty short lifespan

ABOVE: Constructed between 1962 and 1964, the Merrion Centre on Woodhouse Lane was Leeds' first purpose-built shopping centre and one of the first in the UK. Designed by architects Gillinson, Barnett & Allen, it incorporated office blocks, a Mecca ballroom, a Rank cinema, a 42-lane bowling alley and multi-storey parking for 1,100 cars, as well as retail units, cafés and restaurants. It was described as 'a city-within-a-city' by its creators. Woolworth, Tesco, Wimpy, Greenwoods, Hagenbachs and Skanda Grill were among the original tenants. Seen here, on Merrion Street, is a branch of

Stylo. This major British footwear company was run by Leeds-based Arnold Ziff and his family, who had developed the Merrion Centre through their property arm. The 'moving pavement' was unveiled in March 1964 on what appears to have been a typical Leeds spring day. The woman with the pushchair is Marjorie Ziff, Arnold's wife, who performed the formal opening ceremony of the centre on May 26th, 1964. The boy in the pushchair is her son Edward.

ABOVE: From the start, high winds racing through the Merrion Centre caused problems. A roof was added above the main mall within three years of it opening. In the recollections of many Leeds residents, the innovative moving walkways 'never worked' and they were removed in the early 1970s. The 35-yard slope here from Merrion Street was covered over from the mid 1980s and improved as part of the refurbishment programme carried out in 2011. The centre was always slightly removed from the heart of the city's shopping district and in recent years it has become known for its concentration on value or discount retailers, such as Peacocks, Poundworld, Bonmarché, Superdrug, Shoezone and Home Bargains. The child in the pushchair, Edward Ziff, has been chief executive of his family's Town Centre Securities property business since 2001 and chairman since 2004. He estimates the centre attracts around sixteen million visitors each year.

1966

# WADE LANE

The Merrion Centre and its facilities have been updated regularly

LEFT: In 1964 the notion of having shops with leisure facilities in a vehicle-free environment was novel. The *Yorkshire Evening Post* declared the Merrion Centre 'emulated what every successful large town and city wanted to build". Its development was linked to traffic-related planning of the period, which saw the Inner Ring Road laid out to the north of the city centre between 1964 and 1968. Seen in 1966, Wade Lane at the back of the centre turned into Lovell Park Road, which passed over the new urban motorway. The large block in the centre is Wade House. The Merrion Hotel, operated by Rank, was opened by the Duke of Devonshire on January 12th, 1966. The General Wade pub, in a distinctive hexagonal building, can just be seen at the right. The name Wade Lane is unconnected with the eighteenth-century general, as it has been in use since 1677 and celebrates Thomas Wade, a sixteenth-century Leeds philanthropist.

ABOVE: The centre may look as if little has changed in fifty years, but more than £70 million worth of improvements were made between 2013 and 2018. This was part of a phased refurbishment and redevelopment plan that started in 2006. The 11-storey Wade House, which for many years housed the Yorkshire Bank credit card centre, is still a commercial offices block. Rank ran the hotel for about ten years and was succeeded by a number of other operators, most recently Ibis Styles, whose hotel opened in 2017, offering about 130 rooms. The creator of the Merrion Centre, noted Leeds businessman Arnold Ziff, is remembered in Arnold's, a restaurant opened in September 2018 on the site of the old General Wade pub. The district has benefited greatly from the increased business brought in by the First Direct Arena, which was opened just to the north in 2013.

c. 1962

# MERRION STREET / WOODHOUSE LANE

The Merrion Centre, Leeds' first modern shopping complex, was opened here in 1964

LEFT: In 1941 an ancient well was uncovered on the site of the car park on Woodhouse Lane during excavations for a static water basin. This photograph dates from the early 1960s before the Merrion Centre was constructed on the open land. Looking west along Merrion Street towards Woodhouse Lane, the view is dominated by the Millstone Grit edifice of what had been opened in 1889 as Central Higher Grade School. Erected by Leeds School Board as the town's first local authority secondary school, it was renamed City of Leeds School in 1928. By the 1970s, this boys' grammar school was also known colloquially as Leeds Central High. Just beyond it is one of the domes of Thoresby High, its all-girls neighbour. To the left, on Great George Street, is a garage. To the right, on Rossington Street, is what was the Methodist New Connexion Chapel, built in 1857–58, and later used by Leeds College of Music.

ABOVE: After its first phase opened in 1964, the Merrion Centre was extended in 1972 from a 4.5-acre site to one of 6.5 acres by developing land to the north for a Morrisons supermarket. The centre has had periodic refurbishments since, as well as seeing tenants come and go. A marked development in recent years has been the growth in eating establishments, as seen here, with a large pub-restaurant, The Picture House, a Caffè Nero and a KFC. Among other local changes, City of Leeds School was relocated to Woodhouse Moor in 1994. The building was used for council offices until 2018. Conversion into a luxury hotel is one idea for it. The tower at left is called K2, created in 2002 by architects Abbey Holford Rowe improving and re-cladding Dudley House, a 20-storey building from 1972. Apartments and offices are on the upper floors, while the ground-floor leisure and retail units are called The Cube.

c. 1905

# ST ANNE'S CATHEDRAL
## The Roman Catholic cathedral occupies a cramped site thanks to redevelopment work around 1900

LEFT: Built in 1838, St Anne's Roman Catholic church was raised to cathedral status in 1878, but it faced down East Parade and stood in the way of the development of what was to become Cookridge Street. It was compulsorily purchased by the council and demolished between 1899 and 1904. The resulting road layout may have improved traffic flow but it left the new cathedral on this cramped and sloping position at the corner of Cookridge Street and Great George Street to the rear of the previous location. Built by John Henry Eastwood and his assistant Sydney Kyffin Greenslade from 1902 in an Arts and Crafts Gothic style, the new cathedral cost £52,000 (around £6 million in today's values) and saw its first Mass in 1904. Its tower was supposed to have been on the front right-hand corner, but opposition from warehouse owners opposite, on the grounds of loss of natural light, forced it to be positioned on the other side.

RIGHT: One of twenty-four Roman Catholic cathedrals in England and Wales, St Anne's has been Grade II* listed since 1963. In 2005–2006 it received funding from English Heritage and the Wolfson Foundation for major restoration, which cost £2.5 million and closed the church for fifteen months. It was reopened on November 13th, 2006. Included in the refurbishment was the magnificent painted reredos or decorative screen in the Lady Chapel by A. W. Pugin, architect of the Houses of Parliament. Designed in 1842, it was carved in wood by George Myers of Hull, a regular Pugin collaborator. Also cleaned were fourteen paintings of the *Stations of the Cross* by Cesare T. G. Formili, installed in 1912. The organ, built in 1904 for St Anne's by the firm of Norman and Beard, had been unused since the 1970s. It was restored by Johannes Klais in Bonn, Germany, in 2009 and played for the first time again in the cathedral on May 16th, 2010. Seen behind the cathedral is The Cube tower block on Woodhouse Lane.

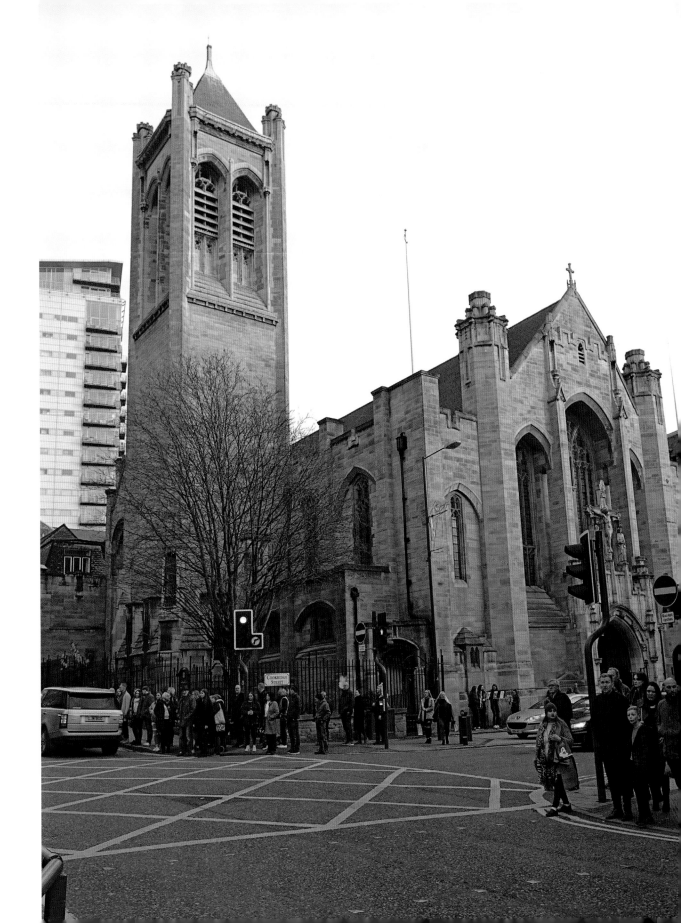

c. 1936

# THE HEADROW / THE LIGHT
The name of the Leeds Permanent Building Society's staff newspaper lives on . . .

LEFT: The main west–east road at the northern edge of the Leeds shopping district, The Headrow, was created as recently as 1928–32. Prior to the road widening of that era, this section was known as Guildford Street. Plans for alterations and improvements were put forward in 1924 and there followed a period of demolishing many old, single-storey shops. Among the new-builds in brick and Portland stone that replaced them were the grand premises of The Leeds Permanent Building Society on the corner of Cookridge Street and The Headrow. Its position put it close to the traditional heart of Leeds' financial district, slightly to the south, but placed it also within the modern development of the city. The building was designed by Sir Reginald Blomfield, who oversaw The Headrow project. Lewis's department store, which opened in September 1932, can be seen on the crest of the slope.

ABOVE: The scene appears little changed between the two photographs, with just different street lights, a few trees and floral planters dividing The Headrow. St Andrew House, the office block nearest the camera on the south side, was renewed in 1977. Next to it, the Mansio Suites accommodation complex is adjacent to The Headrow pub (formerly The Green Dragon). Blomfield's work on the north seems untouched, but the difference is behind the facade. The corner building ceased to be the head office of the Leeds Permanent Building Society in 1992. Between 1999 and 2001 the area behind it was cleared for the construction of The Light, a complex designed by DLG Architects that includes shops, restaurants, a cinema, gym and nightclub. Named after the staff newspaper of the building society, it was opened on November 12th, 2001. The building to the left was converted into the Radisson SAS Hotel, with about 150 rooms. Browns restaurant is on the corner.

# PARK ROW

A street best known for its impressive bank buildings

LEFT: Park Row was laid out in 1776. Most of the buildings here were built in the Victorian era, by which time the street was known as the city's main financial thoroughfare. On the east side, at the junction with Bond Street, is Beckett's Bank. Beckett and Blayds Old Bank was moved here from Briggate when their Gothic revival-style building by George Gilbert Scott – creator of the Albert Memorial in London – was finished in June 1867. The photograph was taken in 1944 and the sign above the entrance promotes Defence Bonds. Beyond Beckett's can be seen the Sun Insurance offices and, with a large clock, the Eagle Star Insurance Company building. The premises on the left were designed by architect Alfred Waterhouse in 1898 for the William Williams, Brown & Co. Bank. Lloyd's Bank moved into the property in 1900. In the distance can be seen the tower of St Anne's Cathedral. Note the traffic lights installed at this junction in 1928, the UK's first permanently operated lights.

ABOVE: Park Row presents an intriguing mixture of old and new. At least twelve properties here are Grade II listed, often because of their lavishly decorated facades. There are modern additions too, notably at No. 15–16, which is the glass-fronted building between two brown ones on the eastern side. Completed in 1997, the 7-storey property has been leased since 2014 to the University of Law Business School, which has four hundred students. With reportedly two hundred-plus law firms, Leeds is reputedly the UK's largest legal centre outside London. As a major commercial street, Park Row retains some banks – HSBC and NatWest face each other here – but the street is equally known today for its varied restaurants and bars. At No. 28–30, the J. D. Wetherspoon pub is named Beckett's Bank. The pub building actually belonged first to Martins Bank, then Barclays.

c. 1961

# MARSHALL & SNELGROVE / BOND STREET
The city's finest department store was replaced by a bank's head office

LEFT: A Yorkshireman by birth, John Marshall opened his first shop in central London in 1837. With John Snelgrove as his partner, he opened a grand department store on London's Oxford Street in 1851. Perhaps because of his northern roots, Marshall set up stores in several Yorkshire locations, including Scarborough, Harrogate, Bradford, Sheffield and York. This one in Leeds was opened in 1870, the year before James Marshall retired, to be succeeded by his son James C. Marshall. The upper floors here were added much later. Financial difficulties caused by a slump in the upmarket department store trade during the First World War forced a merger with Debenhams in 1919, but the original name was retained until the 1970s. Marshall & Snelgrove vied with Leeds-based Schofields to be regarded as the most upmarket of the city's department stores and played on its London connection to emphasise its fashionable credentials.

ABOVE: In the early 1970s, Debenhams closed Marshall & Snelgrove and the building was demolished. In its place appeared a purpose-built 10-storey office block that was to serve as the regional head office for Lloyds Bank. Its largely glass facade was typical of the period. The financial crash of 2008 caused considerable reduction in the property estates of banks and by 2016 the bank had exited and the building was refurbished to reflect the changing uses of city centre sites. The upper floors of the building were modernised to contemporary office standards, while part of the ground floor was meant to be a restaurant and the lower basement a gymnasium, underlining the growth in city-centre leisure and dining. But by late 2018 only one floor of the building was occupied. The neighbouring building nearer City Square, once the site of an architecturally flamboyant branch of National Provincial Bank, is No. 1 Park Row.

1927

# ALBION STREET

Old buildings were swept away just before 1928 for the creation of The Headrow

ABOVE: The picture postcard format was standardised in 1899 to a measurement of 5½ x 3½ inches. In 1902 the British Post Office changed its regulations on the format of postcards and the familiar divided back was permitted, so that the address and a message could be written on it, while the other side could carry a photograph or illustration. This ushered in a craze for sending picture postcards that were the social media of the pre-1945 era. The huge demand for personal portraits kept companies

like Edwin Avison's studio, seen here in Albion Street in 1927, very busy. Contemporary social mores also kept people like John Pickering in work. It was expected in polite society to present your credentials on the *cartes de visite* he produced when being introduced to a new acquaintance. In the background, on what was then Guildford Street, is the Commercial Hotel.

ABOVE: The location was transformed by the creation of the modern Headrow in 1930, when the Commercial Hotel was replaced by part of Sir Reginald Blomfield's masterplan. The building is now part of The Light leisure complex. The corner site where Albion Street meets The Headrow was acquired by the Leeds and Holbeck Building Society for £42,500 and its new head office opened on March 12th, 1930. It was extended down Albion Street in 1963 and along The Headrow in 1970. Founded in 1875, the society dropped 'and Holbeck' in 2003. A stone marker from 1725 for the Burley Bar, one of the medieval gates of the city, is displayed in the reception area. Albion Street illustrates well the changes in use city centre premises have undergone in the past fifty years. In the early 1950s this stretch of the street housed a gun maker, a solicitor, an estate agency and a fashion business.

1949

# SCHOFIELDS / THE CORE

A local success story, Schofields grew into a department store from one small drapery shop

ABOVE: The construction of shopping arcades in city centres was very popular in the last quarter of the nineteenth century and Leeds embraced the trend with remarkable enthusiasm. The first was Victoria Arcade, opened in 1898 to mark Queen Victoria's Diamond Jubilee the previous year. It was laid out in

an L-shape south from Upperhead Row (later renamed The Headrow) to Lands Lane. One of its first tenants, from 1901, was local draper Snowden Schofield. By 1949, when this photograph was taken, his original shop at No. 1 Victoria Arcade had been extended to a number of neighbouring units in the arcade and

adjacent buildings to the west, to form the Schofields department store. Reportedly, Schofield's friend H. G. Shipham liked the arcade location so much that he established his men's outfitting business on the east side of the entrance. The distinctive arch of the arcade was topped off with a glass dome.

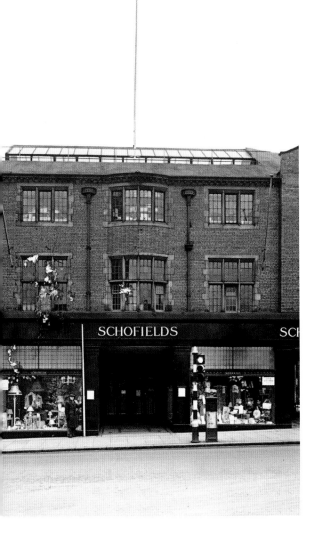

ABOVE: The brightly coloured entrance to the retail and leisure complex, The Core, appears to echo, in a slightly garish manner, the archway of the Victoria Arcade that once stood on the site. But it is hard to believe that the modern building has ever created the excitement of its predecessor. Rebuilt in 1962, the Schofields store ceased trading on the site in 1986, by which time the business was part of the House of Fraser (HoF) group. The 1962 store – seen in the following spread – was demolished in 1987 and replaced by an enclosed shopping centre originally called the Schofields Centre, in which the HoF-owned Schofields had a very small and very short-lived presence. The new centre was not a commercial success and was closed in 1996, refurbished and reopened as The Headrow Centre. This process was repeated in 2010 when the building was remodelled and renamed The Core, with entrances on The Headrow and Lands Lane.

1967

# SCHOFIELDS / THE CORE
Schofields' 1962 store lasted less than thirty years

ABOVE: Despite all the major retail chains being represented in Leeds, significant home-grown businesses retained a market-leading position in the city. In this 1967 view of the crest of The Headrow, looking east, is Schofields department store in its 1962 modernist-style building. Its previous premises, including the Victoria Arcade, were demolished in 1959. The business was viewed as the most upmarket of Leeds department stores despite competition from Marshall & Snelgrove. Seen on the north side of the street is Vallances, a radio and television shop that was best-known for its record department, complete with wall-mounted listening booths. Although many people thought it was a Leeds independent, it was part of a forty-strong chain based in Scunthorpe. Its first shop in Leeds had been on Briggate. The corner of the Lewis's department store can also be seen.

ABOVE: Headrow House is now Direct Line House, one of the two large offices in Leeds for the insurance group. The building, completed in 1955, was the last to be built on the north side of The Headrow and its design was criticised because it did not follow Reginald Blomfield's stylistic template and was taller than its uniform neighbours. This western end of the former Lewis's is a Sainsbury's supermarket, another indication of changing retail use in urban centres. On the south side, we have an example of the folly of retail over-expansion in Leeds, a problem made worse in the past fifteen years by the rise of online sales. The city has too much shopping space, which helps explain the slightly eerie atmosphere in The Core, which uses the slogan, Eat Drink Shop.

# ST JOHN THE EVANGELIST / ST JOHNS CENTRE

The oldest church in Leeds has become hidden by successive retail developments on The Headrow

1978

LEFT: Tucked away off New Briggate is St John the Evangelist, Leeds' oldest surviving church. Consecrated in 1634, it was endowed by John Harrison, an affluent philanthropist who, like many burghers of the city, had made his fortune as a wool merchant. The church Is built of fine-grained sandstone that was quarried from Woodhouse Moor, a mile or so to the north. Grade I listed since 1963, it is described by Historic England as 'a rare Gothic survival building in Perpendicular style'. The upper part of the church tower was replaced by architect John Clark in 1838 and other restorations were made between 1866 and 1868. Among other achievements, Harrison established an old pathway north from Briggate as New Street; it was later renamed New Briggate. He also established a school, later Leeds Grammar School, and built alms houses for poor women alongside St John's. A stained-glass window in the church celebrates his memory, along with Harrison Street alongside the Grand Theatre on New Briggate.

BELOW: Architectural historian Nikolaus Pevsner said St John's was 'the only church at Leeds of more than local interest' but the building has not been used as a place of worship since 1975. It is under the care of the Churches Conservation Trust. Just to the north, the small Merrion Street Gardens is one of only six public open spaces in Leeds city centre. Harrison's alms houses, rebuilt in 1850, were demolished in 1960, by which time the church was almost completely obscured from the south by Lewis's and Headrow House. Since 1985, the building has been overshadowed too by St Johns Centre, a small shopping complex designed by Gillinson Partnership that the city planners approved despite the proximity of the Merrion Centre and what is now The Core. The small space in front of the centre is Dortmund Square, named in 1980 to mark the tenth anniversary of Leeds' twinning with the German city.

1898

# LANDS LANE

A busy little street that marked the medieval lord of the manor's boundary

LEFT: The lost art of wall signwriting is superbly shown in this 1898 photograph that looks down the minor street of Lands Lane from what is now The Headrow. T. P. (Thomas) Mallorie & Co's wine and spirits emporium ('Est 1812') dominates the vista. Among its offerings are Courvoisier brandies and Glenlivet whisky, which would be known to today's discerning drinker. The Mallorie store, which was reduced in size when the street was widened and improved between 1898 and 1902, was still trading here in the 1950s. Propped up against Mallorie's wall are decorative mirrors from the large furnishings firm Allpass and Co., which also promoted its organs and pianos on its frontage – ideal for those Victorian musical evenings at home. Allpass's shop was in Thornton's Buildings. On the right is an indication of a new era of development for Leeds retailing – work has commenced on the Victoria Arcade.

ABOVE: Thornton's Buildings, on the left, has been a Grade II-listed building since 1996. The Historic England website reminds us: 'Charles Thornton played a crucial part in the development of Leeds as a shopping centre, developing this corner and Thornton's Arcade.' What would the Victorian entrepreneur make of the changes to Lands Lane, which was pedestrianised in the early 1970s? Further down Lands Lane, the entrance to Thornton's Arcade is well kept, but the Mallorie & Co. building has gone, to be replaced by an ugly concrete construction from the 1960s. Its archway leads to Swan Street, which runs eastwards to the City Varieties and Briggate. Dominating the western edge is the corner unit of The Core shopping complex. At the end of the street is the Trinity Leeds complex and the spire of Holy Trinity Church.

1956

# THORNTON'S ARCADE

Created for entrepreneur Charles Thornton, this was the first of Leeds' celebrated shopping arcades

ABOVE: Although a short and narrow thoroughfare, Lands Lane was witness to several key moments of Leeds' long history. Taking its name from the fields or lands of the medieval Lord of the Manor of Leeds, it marked the boundary of burgage plots, which typically comprised a house and a long narrow strip of land rented from an aristocrat. Alongside what became the street, Red Hall, generally assumed to be the first brick-built house in Leeds, was finished in 1628 as the substantial home of wool merchant

Thomas Metcalfe. This view from July 7th, 1956 shows the layout following the widening of the street in about 1899. Notable is the western entrance to Thornton's Arcade, the first of Leeds' splendid enclosed retailing gems. It was constructed over the former Old Talbot Inn Yard to a design by George Smith for Charles Thornton, who also built the City Varieties and Thornton's Buildings at the northern end of Lands Lane.

ABOVE: More than 140 years after it opened, Thornton's Arcade is still a good draw for shoppers who appreciate independent businesses. The narrowest of Leeds' arcades, with the large paving stones known as 'flags' in Leeds as its flooring, it has been Grade II listed since 1976. It was sensitively restored in 1993 and refurbished externally in 2010. Three storeys high with a glass roof, the arcade has, at this Lands Lane end, a clock made by William Potts and Sons of Leeds. It features characters from Sir Walter Scott's *Ivanhoe*. Richard Coeur-de-Lion and Friar Tuck strike the hours, while Robin Hood and Gurth the Swineherd strike the quarters. The life-size quartet was made by the Leeds sculptor John Wormald Appleyard. On the south end wall is the head of a woman modelled on the painting of the Duchess of Devonshire by Thomas Gainsborough. A copy of the painting was stolen from the arcade soon after it opened.

# QUEEN'S ARCADE

Thanks to the small size of its shops, it has remained a haven for local independent retailers

BELOW: The main entrance to Queen's Arcade on Briggate is decorated with a large clock by Potts of Leeds placed on a bracket over the street. The Lands Lane entrance at the other end, shown here around 1967, is more modest and gives little clue to the fine interior. Designed by London-based architect Edward Clark, the arcade was built by Armistead & Proctor over the Rose and Crown Yard (also known as Binks Hotel), which was itself on the site of one of Briggate's medieval burgage plots. Clark gave the arcade an unusual two-storey galleried layout. On the north gallery was the Queen's Arcade Hotel, while opposite was a balcony of small shops. One tenant when it opened in 1889 was Brown's toy shop, which was still trading there at least until the late 1950s. A more recent arrival was Harry Fenton, a London-based menswear chain that was very popular with Mods. A sign for Levi's jeans can be seen in its window.

BELOW: Lands Lane is a secondary retail location and attracts businesses that want to avoid the high rents of primary positions. Serving as an easy route from The Headrow to Trinity Leeds, it sees plenty of footfall. The buildings on this east side are generally well preserved, with the Queen's Arcade being particularly attractive, painted light blue and white. Grade II listed since 1987, the arcade has eighteen, mainly small retail units that appeal to independent operators, notably jewellery, accessory and fashion retailers. At 11–13 is Accent Clothing, a unisex fashion business founded in 1984 by Martin Schneider, which is a Leeds institution. Unusually for the arcade, Accent has extended backwards and upwards into the roof space to increase its space. Accent was named UK Independent Retailer of the Year in 2018 by leading trade magazine *Drapers*. In a neat link with the past, the former Harry Fenton shop, which sold Levi's, is now occupied by the jeans brand.

# THORNTON'S BUILDINGS

A striking corner site, it has seen many businesses occupy its ground-floor shops

BELOW: On April 5th 1935, Benefit Footwear Specialists occupied the prime corner position of the three-storey Italianate Thornton's Buildings. Only five years earlier, the same spot had been the premises of tailor Louis McKennell. To the left is the impressive unit of Eveleigh Bishop, dealers in silverware, but only three years later it had been replaced by a wallpaper shop and a cooked meats specialist. Further east can be seen The Horse and Trumpet pub, with a sign for local brewer Tetley's. The alley between the pub and Thornton's leads to the City Palace of Varieties theatre, founded in 1865 by pub landlord and entrepreneur Charles Thornton, who also developed this building and Thornton's Arcade. The theatre was originally Thornton's New Music Hall and Fashionable Lounge. Benefit, part of a national chain founded in Hull in 1875 as The Public Benefit Boot Company, had a major footwear repairs factory in Templar Street, Leeds, and also occupied Barran's former warehouse.

1935

BELOW: Charles Thornton picked a good location for his building, as the junction of Lands Lane and The Headrow continues to have a consistent stream of potential customers passing by. The contemporary tenant, The Carphone Warehouse, was founded in 1989 and rode the boom in mobile phone use. Before Carphone Warehouse opened here in 2007, its retail tenants in recent years included fashion chains Jacques Vert and Principles womenswear. Also noticeable in this image is how much more street furniture we have today and how less elegant street lamps are.

1938

# THORNTON'S BUILDINGS / THE HEADROW

It's easy to see how the street-level tenants have changed, but changes on the upper floors are more of a mystery

ABOVE: In 1928, the men's hosier and shirt-maker Edward Skelton had a branch at 13 New Briggate on a block that was demolished for the creation of The Headrow. Here, on September 19th, 1938, we find the same business among the tenants of Thornton's Buildings on the other side of The Headrow. Constructed in 1873 for local entrepreneur Charles Thornton, this impressive block included shops at street level, offices above

(which at this time also housed a women's hairdresser) and top-lit workshops. The sequence of retailers in this little parade from numbers 55 to 65 – optician, pawnbroker, men's outfitter, wallpaper shop and cooked meats purveyor – was typical of the variety of independent shops Leeds offered at the time. Founded in 1801, jeweller Owen & Robinson today trades in Commercial Street, Leeds.

ABOVE: The upper facade of Thornton's Buildings remain remarkably unchanged eighty years later, but at street level, the types of retail businesses are markedly different. These are small shops, only about 12 yards wide, so they have limited appeal to many modern retailers. With three of the five units – Easy Bite, Greggs and Fatso's – selling take-away food, we are reminded how British eating habits have changed over the past thirty years. AZ Nails at No. 61a reflects another more recent consumerist phenomenon: the rise of beauty, cosmetic and 'well-being' retailers satisfying the needs of those who wish to express their personality through their appearance. What is classed as 'Service Retail' (a category that includes nail bars, barbers and tattoo parlours) has been the only one to see consistent growth in numbers of operators, and Leeds city centre reflects this.

1932

# LEWIS'S DEPARTMENT STORE

When it was opened in 1932, Lewis's was the largest department store opened in the UK since Selfridges in London in 1909

ABOVE: A double-page spread in the October 1st 1932 edition of the clothing trade magazine *The Drapers' Record* proclaimed: 'The New Yorkshire Store An Amazing Success'. As a central part of the redevelopment of The Headrow, the Liverpool-based Lewis's department store group (no relation to John Lewis) had built the largest department store since Gordon Selfridge had revolutionised British shopping with his Oxford Street store in 1909. Covering more than 180,000 square feet on a double-height ground floor and first floor, the store had cost £750,000 to build and £250,000 to fit out and stock (about £50 million and £17 million in today's values). Designed by Sir Reginald Blomfield, majordomo of the entire Headrow project, the store was conceived as a 7-storey edifice, but the upper floors were not added until the 1950s. It is seen here soon after its opening.

c. 1925

ABOVE: The reverse view looking east down The Headrow.

ABOVE: The story of Lewis's over the past thirty years encapsulates an era of corporate deal-making, retailing over-optimism and shifts in shopping habits. By 1965 Lewis's was part of the Sears Group, controlled by retail entrepreneur Charles Clore. In 1991, after the break-up of Sears, Lewis's went into administration and was bought by Owen Owen, another department store group. The Leeds store closed in February 1991. In 1996 it reopened as a branch of London-based store group Allders, which itself went bust in 2005. In May 2005 the building ceased to be used as a department store. In 2007 a £36 million scheme was approved to redevelop the building and Primark took most of the retail space. In March 2015 Primark moved its Leeds presence to the Trinity shopping centre. Sainsbury's, TK Maxx, TK Maxx's Home Sense subsidiary and Argos now occupy the ground floor. The office block on floors 2–6 is called Broad Gate.

1949

## ODEON CINEMA
Opened as a Paramount cinema, its vast auditorium seated 3,600 people

LEFT: As part of Sir Reginald Blomfield's redevelopment of The Headrow in the late 1920s and early 1930s, milliner and furrier H & D Hart had to relocate to Briggate from its position at the corner of New Briggate and Lowerhead Row. In its place on February 22nd, 1932 came the Paramount cinema designed by London architect Frank T. Verity. The stalls seated 2,590, with another 1,010 in the balcony, which perhaps explains why it was promoted as the 'Wonder Theatre of the North'. The Lord Mayor of Leeds, Alderman F. B. Simpson, performed the opening ceremony and the audience left the new attraction to the strains of the Yorkshire dialect favourite, *On Ilkla Moor Baht 'At*, played by Rex O'Grady on a £20,000 Wurlitzer organ. Despite this bold launch, the American-owned Paramount chain was taken over by Odeon Theatres in November 1939 and the Leeds branch was renamed Odeon in April 1940. It is seen here in 1949.

ABOVE: This corner of The Headrow and New Briggate has become a centre for discount retailing. The Odeon cinema closed in 2001 and the huge building was originally to be converted to an apartment and leisure complex. It was acquired by discount fashion chain Primark, which converted it into a three-storey store that opened in August 2005. Primark stayed until 2015, when it consolidated its Leeds stores into a single branch in Trinity Leeds. Since July 2015 the 45,000-square-foot site has been occupied by discount fashion retailer Sports Direct and its young fashion subsidiary USC, which trade across the basement and three upper floors. There are one or two other small tenants at the eastern end of the building, but that stretch of The Headrow is not prime retail space. As a non-retail footnote, the mighty Wurlitzer from the cinema is part of the Thursford Collection, near Fakenham, Norfolk.

# UNIVERSAL FURNISHING COMPANY / NEW BRIGGATE

Despite its Tudor overtones, the block was built in 1901 and survived until 1967

c. 1908

LEFT: Taken very early in the twentieth century, this view shows the top end of New Briggate, the north-east extreme of the city centre shopping district. On the corner of Merrion Street and Cross Belgrave Street is The Wrens Hotel, which was opened in 1880 by one Alfred Wren. The striking half-timbered shops in the centre, dominated by the Universal Furnishing Company, were constructed in 1901. By the late 1930s, the furniture store had been rebranded as Rothwells, a name that is displayed on a small advertising hoarding on the building here. On the right of the image we can just make out the striking arched entrance of The Grand Arcade, which had been opened in 1897. Faced with impressive Burmantofts glazed terracotta tiles, by local architects Smith & Tweedale, this most northerly of the city's famous arcades had a somewhat plain interior. It comprised two parallel arcades running down to Vicar Lane, with a cross passage linking it to Merrion Street. The adjacent Grand Theatre is just out of this shot.

BELOW: 'Leeds: motorway city of the seventies' was a slogan used for franking mail at the beginning of that decade. In 1972 the M1 reached the city with the opening of the Leeds South Eastern Motorway (now the M621). As early as 1951 a report suggested an inner ring road through Leeds was desirable, but work was not started until 1964. The project was not finished until 2009. The timber-framed buildings shown opposite were demolished in 1967 as part of Stage 2, which brought the A64 York Road sweeping around the north of the city centre. Today, New Briggate continues north over the top of the A64(M), as it is now styled. The five-storey red brick building in the distance, on a corner site at the start of North Street, is Centenary House from 1904, a former public dispensary for the Leeds Society for Deaf and Blind People (later a health centre) that has been converted into residential and commercial units.

c. 1966

# THE GRAND ARCADE

Featuring Burmantofts faience tiles that were perfectly suited to a grimy Victorian city

LEFT: The Renaissance-inspired decorative entrance to The Grand Arcade is far more memorable than its distinctly plain interior, which has a simple glazed roof and no balconies, unlike the larger arcades further down Vicar Lane. The exterior of the structure, designed by Smith and Tweedale in 1897, is notable for the use of salt-glazed ceramics, known as Burmantofts faience. This attractive architectural facing material was manufactured in the nearby Burmantofts district by The Leeds Fireclay Co., which was owned by James Holroyd. He realised that the faience quality, also known as terracotta, would be relatively easy to clean in the grimy atmosphere of Victorian cities. The condition of the tiles, as seen here in the mid 1960s, shows he was right. The work of another celebrated Leeds specialist firm, clockmaker William Potts and Sons, is seen at this Vicar Lane end of the arcade in a large mechanical timepiece that features a medieval castle protected by knights.

RIGHT: The Grand Theatre, opened in 1878 and home of Opera North for forty-plus years, is a vibrant neighbour of The Grand Arcade, which has not fared so well in the recent past. Its position at the northern edge of the Leeds shopping centre left it as something of a backwater until it was refurbished in 1992. Today, it is a quiet haven for an eclectic mix of independent businesses. The Tower Picture House was part of the arcade from 1920 until 1985 when it was succeeded by a discotheque, then a bar. A large ghost sign for Tower is on the exterior Merrion Street wall. It is hard to imagine the arcade, which was Grade II listed in 1985, ever being vibrant again. As the slogan under the Potts' clock warns: *Time and tide wait for no man.*

1898

# BLACK SWAN INN / 1 EASTGATE

The slum clearances of the late nineteenth century saw the famous pub demolished

LEFT: The rapid growth of Leeds as an urban centre in the second half of the nineteenth century resulted in large areas of slums, which became a civic embarrassment. The area around the Black Swan public house, situated on the corner of Vicar Lane and Lady Lane, was one such district. Styled the Vicar Lane Improvement Area in photographs from 1898 (like this one) and 1899, the streets were cleared after the council compulsorily purchased buildings and land. The Black Swan, which was mentioned in the *Leeds Mercury* as early as 1809, had at its rear Black Swan Yard, which was the base for a variety of businesses, including joiner and shop-fitter J. S. Wilby (whose sign is on the pub), coach builder Thomas Butler and several tailors. In 1898, the address of the pub was No. 2 North Street, the road that led from the city centre north to Roundhay.

ABOVE: The creation of The Headrow included the construction of 1 Eastgate, or National Deposit House. Originally occupied by Martins Bank, it was one of three identical buildings built for banks on the junction with Vicar Lane. Its future may be in doubt. Between 2012 and 2017 it was covered by a Certificate of Immunity, which assured developers that it would not be statutorily listed or be served with a Building Preservation Notice (BPN) by the local planning authority. The same guarantee was extended to the low brick building behind it. Universally known as the Old Red Bus Station, 100–104 Vicar Lane was built in 1936 for the West Yorkshire Road Car Company, which mainly served routes to outlying towns like Wetherby and to the Yorkshire coast. Closed in 1994 and little used for twenty years, the building became a bar and music venue in 2016, but the site is ripe for redevelopment.

1967

# EASTGATE ROUNDABOUT

The former petrol station makes an unusual market for the eastern end of The Headrow

ABOVE: If the Town Hall marked the western end of The Headrow, a less impressive structure balanced it at the eastern end. In the section down the slope from Vicar Lane, the wide road is renamed Eastgate but its buildings still follow the plan laid down by architect Sir Reginald Blomfield's masterplan. The end point was Eastgate Roundabout, the location of a hexagonal petrol station built in 1932 to Blomfield's design, long before city planners seemed to have declared war on motorists. In this 1967 shot, it is a BP station run by local motor dealer Appleyard. Just seen at left, with the chimney, is the Union Street swimming pool, public baths and wash house. One of the unmistakeable arches of Quarry Hill Flats, the massive social housing complex, provides the circular framing to this memorable image.

ABOVE: A controversial addition to the Leeds skyline is the patterned, multi-storey car park for Victoria Gate, a glossy shopping centre opened in 2016. Developed by property company Hammerson at a reported cost of £165 million, it marked the conclusion of a planning saga about what should occupy the site largely derelict since Union Street baths was demolished in the early 1970s. The principal architect, Acme, used hundreds of twisting aluminium fins, spaced to allow natural ventilation and daylight in, on the car park's facade. The exterior of the centre's flagship store, John Lewis, created with diagonal struts of etched concrete, can be seen beyond the car park. Five storeys high, this is said to be the tallest post-war department store in the UK outside London. Traditionalists were unhappy that Sir Reginald Blomfield's block on the south side of Eastgate was demolished for Victoria Gate.

c. 1938

# QUARRY HILL FLATS

### The celebrated social housing experiment of the late 1930s

ABOVE AND RIGHT: The Quarry Hill area at the eastern edge of the city centre is regarded as one of the oldest inhabited areas of Leeds. In the 1780s many back-to-back houses were built here and by the 1830s the down-at-heel district was prone to outbreaks of diseases like cholera. By 1910, wholescale slum clearance was proposed, but this did not happen until 1936–38 when Quarry Hill Flats was built. A social housing experiment unique in the UK, this controversial emblem of Leeds was modelled on the Karl Marx complex of workers' flats in Vienna. The first of 3,000 residents moved in on March 30th, 1938. Covering 23 acres and containing 940 flats ranging from five-bedroom units to single-bed flats for elderly residents, Quarry Hill Flats was the largest, most modern flats complex in Europe at the time. All the blocks were named after social reformers from Leeds, such as Oastler House, named for Richard Oastler (1789–1861), a campaigner for better conditions for textile factory workers, especially children. The inset photo shows the nearby bus depot in the late 1950s.

c. 1959

ABOVE: Between 1970 and 1972 Quarry Hills Flats was occasionally featured in the Yorkshire Television sitcom *Queenie's Castle,* which starred Diana Dors and was co-written by Leeds-born Keith Waterhouse. The complex was demolished in 1978 after the discovery of serious structural problems. Since the 1980s, this section of town has become a hub of regeneration. The largest of the new additions is Quarry House, seen on the extreme right, a vast edifice – nicknamed The Kremlin – designed by Building Design Partnership and opened in 1993 as offices for the departments for social security and health. Parts of the NHS are also based here. In front of it, with the sloping roof, is the Leeds Playhouse, built in 1985–90 by the Appleton Partnership when the theatre was relocated from its original home off Woodhouse Lane. The theatre is due to reopen in 2019 after a £15.8 million redevelopment that will add a new entrance and studio. To the left, the blue bridge is part of the Inner Ring Road carrying the A64(M), also known as York Road. Under construction in the centre is the new £57 million Leeds City College campus, scheduled to open in 2019.

1936

# VICAR LANE / NO. 1 THE HEADROW

A rare building on the south side of The Headrow that adheres to Sir Reginald Blomfield's unified style

ABOVE: This image of the junction of Vicar Lane and The Headrow, taken on July 3rd, 1936, was captured five years after the former Lowerhead Row and Upperhead Row – some of Leeds' original streets – had been widened. The buildings on the north side of The Headrow had been demolished. Here we have a fascinating example of the mixture of shops and pubs that contributed to the vibrancy of Leeds' commercial life. The Nag's Head pub is advertising its Concert Room. Two doors away, Hy Wigfall & Son has a window full of 1936-model bicycles. The Phillips footwear corner shop has been vacated. The Waldenberg Bros furniture shop is somewhat overshadowed by the large painted sign above it for its rival Allpass. At the right, we can just see the entrance to Rockley Hall Yard, the front of which had been refaced in 1929. It was named after a residence of John Harrison, the seventeenth-century Leeds philanthropist.

ABOVE: No. 1 The Headrow was the desirable address given to this Barclays Bank building, which follows Sir Reginald Blomfield's uniform frontage plan that so dominates the opposite northern side of the street. The Lloyds Bank building across The Headrow, which was constructed between 1930 and 1932, was the first of three banks-on-corners here. Barclays and Martins, which was built diagonally opposite on the north-east corner of the Vicar Lane-Headrow junction, were both constructed in 1938. An inscription above the door at street level on the west of this Barclays building reads 'Barclays Bank Chambers 1938' and indicates that the entrance is No. 3 The Headrow. Handsome in its own way, this imposing property looks slightly out of place wedged between its older and less grand neighbours, but it provides a visual link with the long run of buildings on the northern side of the street.

# ENTRANCE TO WOOD STREET / VICTORIA QUARTER

The arcades built after slum clearance in the late 1890s were refurbished a century later to create the Victoria Quarter

LEFT: The improvements of the slums near the Black Swan pub around 1899-1900 were on a small scale compared to the work a little further down Vicar Lane. Here, during 1898–1904, the Leeds Estates Company erased the grim slums that surrounded the butchers' slaughterhouses known as the Shambles and neighbouring commercial premises and houses. Probably taken in 1897, this shot shows the entrance to Wood Street through an arch on the west side of Vicar Lane. Among the shops are Whites Medicine Stores at No 17. Next to it is Nobles, which claims to be 'the oldest tool shop in Leeds, founded 1810', and Samuel Saipes, suppliers of tailors' and dressmakers' trimmings. The photograph was taken by the celebrated Wormald of Leeds studio, run by brothers Edmund and Joseph Wormald, who recorded many local buildings.

ABOVE: Despite being a landmark of Leeds, the lavish Victorian arcades designed by architect Frank Matcham and built from 1898 to 1904 between Briggate and Vicar Lane had become somewhat run-down as the 1970s turned to the 1980s. Between 1988 and 1990 a bold programme by the owner, Prudential Assurance, transformed the shabby thoroughfares into the modern Victoria Quarter. As part of this imaginative and highly successful restoration, the former Queen Victoria Street, which separated two of Matcham's blocks, was covered over to unite the arcade buildings on each side. Architects Derek Latham & Co. made no attempt to recreate a Victorian or Edwardian feel here – the tubular structure and large windows are boldly contemporary, but somehow they work with the highly decorative originals. The Victoria Quarter has changed ownership several times since its lavish restoration, which marked a resurgence in the confidence of Leeds. It has become one of the symbols of modern Leeds and current owner Hammerson reckons it attracts 8.5 million visitors a year.

# WOOD STREET / VICTORIA QUARTER

Queen Victoria Street, which replaced the Wood Street yard, was glazed over as part of the 1980s refurbishment

BELOW: Swept away in the slum clearance of 1898—1904 was Wood Street, one of the many enclosed yards running off Briggate that followed the lines of the narrow medieval burgage plots. It had been created by a hatter, Joseph Wood, who combined two yards he had purchased. Running between Briggate and Vicar Lane, it is seen here in its final years, before it was replaced by Queen Victoria Street, the central spine of Frank Matcham's glorious County Arcade development. In this photograph, the rear of the Dolphin Hotel is visible and Vicar Lane can be glimpsed through the arch. In the yard, light engineering firms like tinner W. H. Hodgson and the City Stereotype Foundry were neighbours of at least two pubs, namely the Boy and Barrel Inn, and the Boot and Shoe Inn.

c. 1890

BELOW: The glass roof above the central atrium of the Victoria Quarter, built over the former Queen Victoria Street, is more than 400 feet long. It is decorated with coloured panels created by Oldham-born artist Brian Clarke, who is celebrated for radically updating the medium of stained glass. The composition is the largest single work of stained glass in Great Britain, according to Clarke's website. The edges of the roof were left as clear glass, so that plenty of natural light would penetrate, 'sensitively limiting the amount of coloured light falling onto the polychromatic glazed tiling of (the original) architecture'. Clarke concludes: 'Visitors to the Victoria Quarter are treated to an unforgettable coloured sky. Even during grey autumn afternoons the glass vivifies the space.' The central atrium is designed to encourage visitors to linger and, hopefully, to spend more money in the shops, bars and cafés. The owners of the complex reckon that on average visitors stay or 'dwell' in the quarter for thirty-seven minutes.

1967

# COUNTY ARCADE

The decorative exuberance of architect Frank Matcham's 1904 creation has been painstakingly restored

LEFT AND BELOW: The County Arcade, running from Briggate to Vicar Lane, is a marvellous statement of the self-confidence Leeds demonstrated as the nineteenth century turned into the twentieth. Some 394 feet long in a T-shape, with the bar at the Vicar Lane end, it is extravagantly decorated with marble, Burmantofts faience and mosaics. The arcade was conceived in three sections by architect Frank Matcham and built from 1898 to 1904 on the site of the former Shambles butchers' district and various yards. Originally all the ground-floor shop fronts were of mahogany, while above were balconies on each side and, on top of the cast-iron arched roof, three glass domes. Included in the complex was a Mecca Locarno Ballroom, which was opened on November 3rd, 1938. By 1967, when this image was shot, it had been restyled as The Spinning Disc, the 'Beat Centre' of the North.

1967

RIGHT AND BELOW: The refurbishment of the run-down arcades in the late 1980s was the idea of the then-landlord, Prudential Assurance. Bold in its vision and superb in its execution, the work overseen by architects Derek Latham & Co. included the reconstruction of the marble pilasters between the shops in artificial materials. All the shop fronts were renewed in mahogany with standard name boards of Art Nouveau-style gold lettering on black glass. The Mecca disco was closed in 1969 (after a new venue was opened in the Merrion Centre in 1964, this became known as the Old Mecca). The unit was a café before becoming a fashion shop. Where the passage from Cross Arcade meets County Arcade is one of three beautiful circular mosaics featuring stylised fruit and flower motifs, created by ceramic artist Joanna Veevers. Enhancing the arcade, they make a visible link to the visual arts of the late Victorian/early Edwardian era.

c. 1908

# CROSS ARCADE

The southern edge of the Edwardian arcades housed the first Marks & Spencer shops outside Kirkgate Market

ABOVE: Separate from but integral to County Arcade was Cross Arcade. This richly decorated covered shopping parade ran from King Edward Street across Queen Victoria Street to join County Arcade in the scheme designed by noted theatrical architect Frank Matcham. This jewel in Leeds was one of Matcham's very few creations that was not a theatre or music hall. Where Cross Arcade met County Arcade was a striking glazed cupola, which was said to have been inspired by the 1865 Galleria Vittorio Emanuele II in Milan. Decorating the dome are four mosaics representing aspects of the city's character, namely Liberty, Art, Labour and Commerce. One of Leeds' most famous commercial concerns, Marks & Spencer, took these two units in County Arcade when it was opened in 1904. Michael Marks started his Original Penny Bazaar in nearby Kirkgate Market in 1884; these were his first shops outside the market.

ABOVE: Grade II* listed since 1974, County Arcade and Cross Arcade were integrated as never before by the restoration project of 1988–90, which saw Frank Matcham's creation rebranded as Victoria Quarter. The attention to detail of the restoration is noteworthy. The glass and wrought-iron roof were repaired and repainted, while the pomegranate frieze at the balcony level was picked out in green and orange. *Trompe l'oeil* paintwork mimicked marble on the refurbished pilasters between the shop fronts. Originally real marble, they were repaired or replaced with glass-reinforced plastic. This small area kickstarted a renaissance in Leeds' reputation as a shopping destination. In the twenty-fifth Leeds Architecture Awards in 2013, Latham Architects received the Outstanding Contribution to Architecture & Design in Leeds award for its Victoria Quarter work, which encapsulated the confidence of modern Leeds as well as Matcham's creation did more than a hundred years earlier.

c. 1910

# LEEDS CITY MARKETS

One of the best-loved buildings in Leeds, this 1904 structure succeeded one from 1857

LEFT: Since July 1st, 1904 this flamboyant building has been known as Kirkgate Market, although it is more correctly called Leeds City Markets. It was designed by architects John and Joseph Leeming of Halifax, who won a competition to design a new covered market to replace the one that originated in 1857. Like County Arcade just across Vicar Lane, it represents the exuberant spirit of Leeds in the early twentieth century. The vast new markets building included the later extensions of the previous market. As well as stalls within, the new structure, in a Flemish style with Art Nouveau embellishments, included eighteen shops on the frontage, a hotel, restaurant, billiard hall, coffee room and club facilities. The original estimate for the construction was £73,000 but the final bill was £116,750. A clock by local makers Potts and Sons was positioned in the hall at first but it was removed in 1912 when a central entrance was added on Vicar Lane and the stalls layout was rearranged.

ABOVE: In 1893, the year Leeds was granted city status, the Central Market, close to the Corn Exchange, was destroyed by fire, a calamity that spurred on the decision to build the new Kirkgate Market. On December 13th, 1975, history repeated itself when two-thirds of the market was destroyed by a blaze which produced flames that could be seen 15 miles away. The cause was never identified, although an electrical fault or an overturned paraffin heater have been suspected. No one was injured – stallholders tried and failed to extinguish the fire – but the fire caused £7 million of damage. The 1904 market hall and the top section of the market was undamaged but the lower part east of Vicar Lane, including most of the 1875 stone building, was lost. These were replaced in 1976 and 1981. Further refurbishments were made in 1991, 1995 and 1996. After the 1991 works, Kirkgate Market was upgraded from a Grade II- to a Grade I-listed building.

1901

# THE OLD KIRKGATE MARKET

The old building was pulled down in 1901, while the new one was built in 1981 following the fire of 1975

ABOVE: The road that runs from the town south-eastwards to a large church or kirk (now Leeds Parish Church) was inevitably called Kirkgate. In 1822, fruit and vegetable traders from Briggate relocated to property on Vicar Lane formerly occupied by, appropriately enough, the vicar of Leeds. The cleric was given a new residence at No. 6 Park Row by the town commissioners. A market hall was built for the greengrocers in 1857 and an extension in 1875 brought in butchers from Briggate. Further extensions were added in 1888 and 1898. This covered market has a unique place in British retail history as it was the original location of Marks & Spencer, which opened its first Penny Bazaar here in 1884. The old market hall is seen here in May 1901, immediately prior to demolition, surrounded by advertising hoardings.

ABOVE: This steel wall marks the eastern end of the modern Kirkgate Market, which claims to be the largest indoor market in Europe. There are three hundred stalls and up to 50,000 people visit the market on a Saturday. Additionally, an open-air market is held between the building and the bus station to the east. This end of the market was constructed in 1981 as the second stage of the rebuilding after the great fire of 1975. From Vicar Lane eastwards, the market now comprises the 1904 hall, then the small remaining part of the 1875 hall, which leads to the 1976 hall and the 1981 hall. The market is open from Monday to Saturday, including Wednesday afternoons, which traditionally was half-day closing. Periodic improvements have been made since 1981. Still hugely popular with Leeds residents, the interior of Kirkgate Market has lacked its visual impact following the 1975 fire and its subsequent piecemeal refurbishment. Marks & Spencer has a nostalgic stall in the market to celebrate its debut there in 1884.

1863

## ROTATION OFFICE YARD / NEW MARKET STREET

One of the many narrow yards in the centre of Leeds, it housed an amazing variety of enterprises

LEFT: Typical of the many yards that were crammed in between Briggate, Vicar Lane and Kirkgate, Rotation Office Yard was a narrow close that housed an eclectic set of tenants, many of them specialist manufacturers. The Rotation Office was used by magistrates to handle routine matters. Established on Call Lane in 1775, by 1796 it was upstairs in a house in Kirkgate, with the Leeds Library on the ground floor. Among the tenants here, in what is believed to be 1863, are C. T. Tiffany, brushmaker of No. 118 Kirkgate, tailor and draper Richard Bowman, and William Kirk Duxbury, who is listed in contemporary directories as a manufacturer of bricks and of corsets and stays. Other firms listed in the yard include a bookseller and printer, a plumber and gasfitter, a pawnbroker, and a confectioner and fruit merchant. The poster advertising a waxworks is thought to relate to Allsop's Royal Collection of Wax Work Figures, which between March and April 1863 was at the Music Hall at No. 12 Albion Street.

RIGHT: The triangle between New Market Street, Kirkgate and Call Lane is known to many Leeds residents because several bus routes pass here. The dimensions of the island were probably laid out in the early 1890s. The former London and Midland Bank, later Trustee Savings Bank, then a Lloyds TSB, at No. 110 Kirkgate (its barred windows are seen here) was designed by William Bakewell. It has been Grade II listed since 1995. It is now an amusements arcade, which may sum up modern life to some. The location is between Kirkgate Market and the earlier Central Market building on Duncan Street, which was destroyed by fire in 1893, leading to road widening in the vicinity. Markets attract pubs. The Regent, a Tetley's house whose rear is seen, has been on this spot (now No. 109 Kirkgate) since at least 1822. Until the early 1960s its neighbour at No. 107 was The Mason's Arms, another Tetley's pub. It is now a hair salon.

1956

# NEW MARKET STREET FROM THE CORN EXCHANGE

Well known to many Leeds residents as so many tram and bus routes have passed this spot over the years

ABOVE: Boar Lane and Vicar Lane and their short extensions form distinct boundaries on the south and east sides of the city centre. Strictly speaking, the road to the right here is New Market Street, while just out of shot to the left is Duncan Street. Where they converge, just outside the Corn Exchange, is one of the relatively few island sites in the centre that is not built on. Given its high volume of consumers catching public transport, it was traditionally a good secondary location for retailers. Seen here on

August 31st, 1956, the prominent white building in the centre is a branch of Hepworths, the Leeds-based tailoring business founded in 1864 by Joseph Hepworth. In the 1880s, with his factory in Wellington Street employing 500 people, Hepworth took the unusual step of opening shops to sell his wares directly to the public. Hepworth was Lord Mayor of Leeds in 1906.

ABOVE: In 1893, fire destroyed the Central Market, which stood close to the Corn Exchange. As well as spurring on the decision to build the 1904 Kirkgate Market building, the calamity provided the opportunity to link Vicar Lane with Duncan Street. This little corner of land has long been a busy spot. Its function as a transport hub has changed little between the two photographs, although the buses' liveries have altered, the bus shelters have been upgraded, the trams' overhead cables have gone, the street lamps have been renewed and lots of double yellow lines have appeared. The town planners' preference for planting urban trees can be noted. The location has dropped out of favour with major retailers too. There is no significant chain's name visible in this image and the presence of two charity shops on the short parade on the west side indicates the lack of vitality in this little corner of Leeds city centre.

1906

# THE THIRD WHITE CLOTH HALL

A small part of one of the most important buildings of Georgian Leeds is tucked away behind the Corn Exchange

ABOVE: This unprepossessing fascia, seen here in 1906, had once been the entrance to one of Leeds' most important buildings, the Third White Cloth Hall. Opened around 1775–6, it was the venue for weavers to sell undyed cloth – 'white' in textile jargon – each Tuesday and Saturday. Five indoor streets surrounding a substantial central courtyard housed 1,213 stalls. One of the primary social venues of Georgian Leeds, the Assembly Rooms, was adjacent to the hall. The complex straddled Assembly Street and Crown Street. The cupola here was reportedly from the Second White Cloth Hall

on Meadow Lane, which dated from 1756; the first, from 1711, had been on Kirkgate. The significance of the hall declined in the later nineteenth century as the textile industry became more industrialised. It closed in 1865 to make way for a new railway viaduct leading to the city station. The frontage was the only survivor as the location was taken over by engineering workshops and, as here, dealers in margarine. This image was shot by Hunslet-born photographer Alf Mattison (1865–1944), a famous chronicler of Leeds scenes.

ABOVE: Leeds station is a short distance to the west and the power line gantry to the right serves the railway line that brought about the demolition of most of the Third White Cloth Hall. The brick building beyond is part of Chancellor Court at 21 The Calls, an office building constructed in the early 1990s as part of the revitalisation of the waterfront. The hall was refurbished by John Lyall Architects around the same time and has become one of a clutch of eateries and bars around and behind the Corn

Exchange. The hall today sits on a cramped triangular site edged on the south side by boarded-up railway arches. Tricky to reach by car or lorry, this is not a versatile location and the opportunities for redevelopment seem limited. Grade II* listed since 1951, it remains a unique historical curiosity. Just along Crown Street is the Grade II-listed Waterloo House, all that remains of the Georgian Assembly Rooms.

# THE CORN EXCHANGE FROM DUNCAN STREET

For some, this building by Cuthbert Brodrick is an even greater architectural triumph than his Town Hall

BELOW: Five years after his majestic Town Hall was opened, on July 28th, 1863, architect Cuthbert Brodrick gave Leeds a second iconic building with the opening of the new Corn Exchange. Its direct inspiration was the Halle au Blé (also Corn Exchange) in Paris, which was opened in 1767 and had an iron dome added in 1811. Brodrick's vision was a replacement for the previous Corn Exchange at the northern end of Briggate, which had become too small for the volume of trade. The structure is a free-standing building comprising a basement, a central trading floor surrounded by two levels of balconies and an expansive dome. Some 190 feet long, 136 feet wide and 86 feet high from basement to dome, the Leeds Corn Exchange is regarded, notwithstanding the Town Hall, as Brodrick's masterpiece. In addition to corn merchants, the venue housed offices for many types of commercial firms.

c. 1910

BELOW: Close to the City Markets and the White Cloth Hall that is behind it, the Corn Exchange's location made good business sense in the 1860s, but a hundred years later the building was barely used and was falling into disrepair. It was saved by a major restoration programme in 1989–90 carried out by architects Alsop & Lyall that saw the building cleaned externally and internally converted into a shopping centre for small, independent operators. A huge circle was cut through the ground floor to open up the basement, which had been used for storing grain. New staircases and balustrades that matched Brodrick's designs were installed and the fifty-six original offices became a similar number of retail units. Details like name boards, sample trays and merchants' desks were retained. Despite the excellence of the concept, the centre has never really been a success. In 2018 more work was done to upgrade the basement into a new eating and gathering space called the Kitchen Yard. The building has been Grade I listed since 1951.

c. 1936

# DUNCAN STREET AND BRIGGATE JUNCTION
A busy crossroads at the southern end of Leeds' busiest shopping street

LEFT: It's the mid-1930s and Duncan Street, running west from the Corn Exchange, is a mass of pedestrian and vehicular movement. The image shows the variety of architectural styles that sit together in the centre. The oldest is of Holy Trinity Church, whose spire is seen to the right. Built of stone from nearby Meanwood Quarry in 1722–7 for the fashionable merchant class of the district, it is one of the few buildings to survive the Victorian regeneration of Leeds. At the corner of Boar Lane and Lower Briggate, the former Temperance Hotel, built between 1866 and 1870 for clothing magnate John Barran by Thomas Ambler, is in a distinctly French Second Empire style. Across the road is the unmistakeable frontage of a Montague Burton store. The No. 16 tram on the extreme right carries an advertisement for the *Leeds Mercury*, a newspaper first published in 1718. Around the time of this picture, its office was just off Duncan Street.

ABOVE: Trams have not run in Leeds since 1959. The traffic island and traffic lights indicate a stricter control of vehicular flow. Most of the buildings are largely unchanged. Holy Trinity Church has services twice a week, but it is more used as a community arts centre. In January 2013, the interior was refurbished, new toilets built, its café was upgraded and all its pews were removed. Of the shops, Burton Menswear at 152–154 Briggate had become a branch of Jackson Tailors by 1970. Nando's, the South African-owned chicken restaurant chain, opened in 2006, succeeding the Freewheel cycle shop as a tenant. By 2018 Nando's had seven branches in Leeds, underlying the growth in inexpensive dining out. Another sign of the times is Russell Eaton, a Yorkshire beauty salon operator, occupying the large corner site at 4–6 Boar Lane, also known as Trevelyan Chambers. In the post-war period it had been used by menswear retailers like 50 Shilling Tailors and Alexandre Menswear.

c. 1920

# HEPWORTHS BUILDING ON DUNCAN STREET

The masterpiece of the prolific Leeds architect Percy Robinson, renowned for his decorative style

LEFT: Previously Fleet Street, Duncan Street was renamed after 1797 to celebrate the victory in that year of Admiral Adam Duncan over the Dutch at Camperdown. This four-storey confection of shops and offices above, designed by Percy Robinson, opened around 1904. Decorated with ornamental swags, scrolls and other high-relief panels, it is faced with terracotta from The Leeds Fireclay Co. The prominent tenant is the Leeds-based menswear manufacturer Hepworths, with Home & Colonial Stores, an early grocery chain, its neighbour on Briggate. On the first floor is Walker & Hall, a silverware specialist founded in Sheffield in 1845. Here, probably in the 1920s, the building is topped out with electric signs for Nestle's and Schweppes Ginger Ale. At No. 5 Duncan Street is Milnes the pork butcher with a beautiful sign above its window. At No. 7 is Rawcliffes, which supplied uniforms for Leeds' better schools for decades. Founded in 1897, the business moved to Duncan Street around 1904 and remained here for about a hundred years.

RIGHT: This entire block was Grade II listed between 1992 and 1996, but the condition of the fabric of the building above street level varies somewhat. Looking particularly neglected is No. 7, which has outbreaks of foliage clearly visible on its upper floors. In 1992 the former Rawcliffes building had some of its parapets, swags, console brackets and globes rebuilt, but it is again in need of love and attention. Like many parts of central Leeds, this stretch of Duncan Street has suffered as its retail units are neither large enough nor the correct proportions for most modern large businesses.

c. 1865

# BOAR LANE BEFORE AND AFTER WIDENING
A typically bold Leeds redevelopment plan saw the south side of Boar Lane demolished around 1869

LEFT: Unrecognisable to modern eyes, this is the view westwards down Boar Lane from Briggate before the significant improvement scheme of 1869–1876 was carried out. Only Holy Trinity Church's spire on the right gives us a significant bearing point. During the works, Boar Lane was widened from the 21 feet we see here to 66 feet, with all the buildings on the south side being demolished. As can be deduced by the prosperous-looking retail establishments here, Boar Lane was a popular shopping area for the middle classes. John T. Beer, occupying what was 32 Briggate, circulated volumes of his poetry to promote his tailoring business. His neighbours across Boar Lane were The Central Shawl and Mantle Warehouse of Charles Pullan at No. 33, and at 34 & 35, Edward Bissington, a hatter and hosier. After the widening of the road, this area also attracted several fruit, game and fish dealers that appealed to a clientele who did not want to visit the more plebeian Leeds markets.

ABOVE: For about a hundred years the site that has been occupied by McDonald's since 1986 was known as Saxone's Corner. It was named after the prominent footwear shop opened in 1908; one of the first branches of Saxone, a company formed in that year by the merger of Scottish firms Clark & Co. and F. & G. Abbott. Named after an own-brand sold by Abbott, Saxone became one of the UK's biggest footwear retailers. This shop was closed in the late 1970s or early 1980s. In a bizarre sequence, the old corner site was demolished and replaced with a modern unit in the early 1960s, which was itself knocked down in 1982 to be replaced by today's structure, which is a replica of the Victorian edifice. The adjacent white building, No. 71 Boar Lane, formerly known as Trinity House, dates from around 1870 and has been Grade II listed since 1996. It was for many years the premises of John Jones, costumiers and furriers.

c. 1867

# SOUTH END OF BRIGGATE / TIME BALL BUILDING

Dyson the jeweller closed in 1990 but its remarkable building remains a Leeds landmark

ABOVE: Seen in or about 1867, the spire of Holy Trinity Church soars above the lowly and ramshackle retail establishments of the southern end of Briggate. At the extreme right on the north side of Boar Lane we see the name of Pullan on the shawl and mantle warehouse at No. 33. The business on the opposite corner at No. 32, sporting the sign of a golden star, is the clothier John T. Beer. Pickard, merchant for wine, spirit, ale and tobacco, occupies several units as we travel south, and finally the Boot & Shoe Depot is advertising reductions. All these buildings, dating from the late sixteenth and seventeenth centuries, when this area was a popular residential area for wealthy merchants, were demolished to allow the widening of Boar Lane soon after this photograph was taken.

1973

RIGHT: Built just after the Then photo was taken, 25–26 Briggate is called Time Ball Buildings, but most Leeds people call this Dyson's. Established in 1865, jeweller and watchmaker John Dyson & Sons moved into No. 26 (the northerly unit) in 1872 and by 1890 the firm occupied the entire space. The large clock, flat against the front, dates from when the business occupied Nos. 25 and 26. The gilded time ball mechanism was installed in 1910, along with the higher clock featuring Father Time and the message *Tempus Fugit*. Linked to Greenwich, the ball dropped at precisely 1pm each day. Many couples met for their first date 'under the Dyson's clock'. Dyson's closed in 1990 and the building was restored in 1993, earning it the City of Leeds Annual Design Award in 1994. The building backs on to and is part of the Marriott Hotel, which opened in 2003, partly in the former Temperance Hotel building. For a time the shop space, which retains many Victorian and Edwardian period details, housed the hotel's Georgetown Restaurant. Since 2010 it has been the venue of the hotel's AM Kitchen and Bar Indian restaurant.

1967

# THE C&A BUILDING / TRINITY LEEDS ON BOAR LANE

The Dutch clothing chain traded in Leeds from 1929 until 2001, predating the city's most successful shopping centre

ABOVE: Post-war Baby Boomers will remember the C&A clothing store that was a neighbour to Holy Trinity Church on the north side of Boar Lane, but only a handful will remember The Grand Pygmalion, a department store that occupied the site from 1888. Run by Alexander Monteith of Monteith, Hamilton and Monteith, it was promoted as 'the most complete general drapers shop and house furnishers in Yorkshire'. The store was sold in 1927 and shortly afterwards was demolished. C&A was founded as a trading company in 1841 by Dutch brothers, Clemens and August Brenninkmeijer. Using their first initials, they opened the first C&A store, in Sneek, in the Netherlands, in 1861. Their first British store was opened in London in 1922 and the company opened in Leeds on September 19th, 1929, on the site of the Grand Pygmalion at 63–65 Boar Lane. The store here is seen around 1967.

ABOVE: After almost forty years the European-styled C&A store was demolished and replaced by a rather dull brown-brick building with almost no windows, in November 1970. In 2000, C&A announced its exit from the UK; by 2001 all its British stores were shut. (It had a branch in the White Rose shopping centre in Beeston, too, from 1997.) Fashion chain Next ran a clearance shop in the unit for a time, but the entire block was demolished for the creation of Trinity Leeds, the huge centre which opened in 2013.

It dominates city centre retailing, stretching from Briggate to Lower Basinghall Street and from Commercial Street to Boar Lane. The pale-coloured building at the entrance is occupied by US lifestyle retailer Urban Outfitters. The properties on the block to the west are Grade II listed as 'part of the important group surviving on the north side of Boar Lane from the reconstruction of the street from 1869'.

c. 1936

# NORTH SIDE OF BOAR LANE

Thomas Ambler's Gothic buildings were lost to 1970s redevelopment

LEFT: Boar Lane follows the route of a medieval path that linked Briggate to Leeds manor house, a fortified settlement located near the site of the Scarborough Hotel pub on Bishopgate Street. The buildings we see here were developed by clothing magnate John Barran. He commissioned local architect Thomas Ambler to design most if not all the buildings, starting in the west with the Griffin Hotel and finishing with the Temperance Hotel at the corner of Briggate. The project cost £60,000. In this shot from September 1936, we have a glimpse of some dining options for the better-off in Leeds. At No. 52 the Jacomelli restaurant offered 'Fresh Oysters Daily'. A. Davy of No. 53 handled fine provisions (presumably with same-day delivery in its liveried van). York Café (which specialised in vegetarian and fish dishes) was on the first floor for luncheons and dinners.

ABOVE: Thomas Ambler's Gothic-style buildings on the south side of Boar Lane were saved from demolition in the mid-1970s by the last-minute intervention of conservationists. The north side block was not so lucky, being pulled down at the time to make way for the Bond Street Centre, which was constructed between 1974 and 1977 to a design by John Brunton & Partners. The Victorian buildings had survived for around a hundred years without significant improvement. Their replacement has been updated twice in barely forty years. The Bond Street Centre was overhauled in 1995–96 to be reopened as Leeds Shopping Plaza. Between 2011 and 2013 it was remodelled again as part of the Trinity Leeds shopping centre development and is now known as Trinity West. A glass walkway across Albion Street is part of its modern configuration.

c. 1933

# BRIGGATE LOOKING NORTH FROM BOAR LANE
The most important shopping street in Leeds was laid out as early as 1207

LEFT: A scene from the early 1930s shows Briggate, Leeds' premier shopping thoroughfare, at its bustling best. Motorists have to negotiate trams on both sides of the road and numerous parked vehicles, especially on the western side. On the central island are tram and bus shelters. A notable recent construction on the east side is the four-storey building for F. W. Woolworth – identified by its pale frontage – which was opened on December 1st, 1928. Built on the site of the old Albion Hotel to succeed the first Leeds Woolies that had been opened in 1911, two buildings away at 131 Briggate, it had two sales floors, a second-floor café and a third-floor stockroom. In 1938, Woolies bought the adjacent Victory Hotel to expand the store. Opposite the Victory, the marquee for the Rialto at No. 47 can be seen. Built in 1911 as the Picture House, it changed its name in 1927.

ABOVE: There are apartments as well as offices in No. 148 Briggate, Percy Robinson's flamboyant building at the corner of Duncan Street, but the story of modern Briggate is about shops. The next building, now called Central Arcade, appeared in 2012, built on top of what had been Market Street Arcade since 1930. Locals referred to this narrow cut-through from Briggate to Central Road as 'Leeds' grottiest arcade'. Its modern incarnation has space for small boutiques. The next flat-fronted building is on the site of Woolworths, which closed in 1987. It was temporarily the home of Schofields while the Schofields Centre on The Headrow was being built. In 1989 it opened as Rackhams, part of the House of Fraser group, and was rebranded as House of Fraser in October 1996 as the company phased out its regional sub-brands. The tall building beyond, at 133–137 Briggate, is the Grade II-listed former Post Office Exchange, another Percy Robinson design, from 1907.

# WOOLWORTH BUILDING ON BRIGGATE

The eastern side of Briggate is an interesting mix of old and new buildings

BELOW: About thirty years after the preceding archive photo, the modern town planners have cleaned up Briggate, for better or worse. The trams, tramlines and overhead cables disappeared from Leeds in 1959, the year that the new building for F. W. Woolworth was unveiled. The branch at 131 Briggate had been the American company's fifth outlet in the UK, underlining Leeds' importance as a retailing centre. The new store seen here stretched back from Briggate to Central Road and occupied the site of the 1928 store and the Victory Hotel that had stood next door. Although Woolworths demolished the hotel in 1939, the war intervened and prevented it from developing the site until 1959, which was the company's Golden Jubilee year. By the time this photograph was taken in the late 1960s, the city centre was being dominated by national chains like the Leicester-based footwear name Easiephit and the Liverpool-based Littlewoods, which was at 122 Briggate.

c. 1968

BELOW: Briggate was completely pedestrianised from The Headrow to Boar Lane in 1997 and for many Leodensians the central thoroughfare lost much of its bustling attraction. To the left the large Topshop/Topman unit is one of the anchor stores of Trinity Leeds, the complex conceived by property company Land Securities and designed by Chapman Taylor. Just beyond, at No. 47, it is the central Leeds flagship of Marks & Spencer, which occupies the site of the old Rialto cinema. Completed in 1940, the store was requisitioned by the Ministry of Works during World War II and not opened until 1951. From 1909 M&S had been at 76 Briggate. The prominent statue is called *Minerva* and was commissioned in 2013 by Land Securities from sculptor Andy Scott, who is best known for his horse head statues, *The Kelpies*, in Falkirk. His companion piece to *Minerva*, another equestrian model, *Equus*, is inside Trinity Leeds.

c. 1970

# COMMERCIAL STREET

The small shop units in this secondary location have become particularly popular with jewellers in recent years

ABOVE: Although very much a secondary thoroughfare, Commercial Street has lived up to its name by attracting all manner of retail, catering and service-providing tenants over the years. Photographs from different eras of this street, which runs west–east between Albion Street and Briggate, reveal a constant change in names and fascias. Like much of central Leeds, the retail units are relatively small and so attract businesses that require only a compact space. In this view from the very early 1970s, footwear chains are prevalent, with Ravel Shoes, Manfield and Stead & Simpson all on the south side. There is a reminder, too, that electrical retailer Dixons was previously known as a camera specialist. And there is another sign of 'progress' here; Commercial Street was one of Leeds' first pedestrianised zones in the 1970s.

ABOVE: Major retailers that require large shops are well served by Trinity Leeds, the vast shopping centre just south of Commercial Street. Here, the small shop spaces in the nineteenth-century properties are more suited to businesses selling small items, such as mobile phones – Carphone Warehouse, Virgin and EE are all seen in this image. Even more striking is the concentration of upmarket jewellers in this short stretch. Berry's, a Leeds-based family-owned firm founded in 1897, has a run of shops at

Nos. 44–46, while next door Prestons, which was established in Bolton in 1869, operates a Rolex franchise. Opened in 2012 as the first standalone shop for the Swiss watch brand outside London, this reflected the prosperity of the city. A Rolex spokesman said at the time of the opening: 'Leeds is an affluent, vibrant city that does not seem to have suffered as some have during the recession.'

1928

# KIRKGATE BETWEEN BRIGGATE AND VICAR LANE
There have been quite a lot of retailing twists and turns on this short street

ABOVE: To allow Leeds residents 'to maintain and develop their civic heritage' the council organised a Civic Week between 22nd and 29th September 1928. Banners, bunting, garlands and flags of many European nations decorated the main streets. Among the slogans promoted were 'Leeds Leads' and 'Capital of the North'. Highlighting the city's economic and social achievements, bus tours took citizens to see the new housing developments in the suburbs, while council departments, major employers like Montague Burton, and schools and colleges held open days. The Leeds City Police

Band performing daily concerts in City Square were among the musical attractions. The Queen's Arcade was decorated in a Japanese style for the week, while Kirkgate, between Briggate and Vicar Lane just across from the City Markets, was decorated as Chinatown, as shown here. On the right is Hitchens Service House, a fancy draper that occupied the large corner site on Briggate. The sign for its Cyprus café can just be seen.

**ABOVE:** This city short-cut has plenty of points of interest. At left, the Debenhams store dates from 1936 when it was run by Matthias Robinson, a Hartlepool-based department store group. It opened in Leeds in 1914 on the same site and expanded by acquiring the neighbouring business of milliner and furrier H. & D. Hart. Matthias Robinson was acquired by Debenhams in 1962 and the store was renamed in 1972. The building retains some lovely Art Deco details, especially on the windows. Another Art Deco building, the former Golden Cock Inn, is on the left at No. 13. It is fronted above street level in white Marmo (a type of imitation marble) and decorated with bright blue tiles. It is now a branch of Superdrug. On the right here, where Hitchens stood in the 1920s, is a 1971 block built for Littlewoods, which moved into the location in 1952. Marks & Spencer occupied it briefly in the late 1990s. Since 2001 it has been a branch of Zara, with the entrance at 127 Briggate.

c. 1936

# KARDOMAH CAFÉ

For almost sixty years from 1908, this café, part of a national chain, was a popular meeting point for Leeds residents

LEFT: The Kardomah Café, at 65–66 Briggate on the block just north of Albion Place, was one of Leeds' most popular refreshment stops. It operated from 1908. Despite its exotic name, the national chain had originated in Liverpool in 1844; the Kardomah name was first used in 1887. It sold loose teas and coffees as well as dispensing hot beverages. In this mid-1930s view, the long-standing branch of men's outfitters Horne Brothers, one of a small national chain, can just be seen on the left. In 1937, the womenswear shop Bon Marché closed down and the site, which was known as Bon Marché Chambers, was taken by Philips Furnishing Co. The final unit is occupied by The Great Universal Stores, which had been founded as a mail order company in Manchester in 1900. By the 1930s it was the largest mail order company in the country with its Great Universal and John England catalogues.

ABOVE: This branch of the Kardomah Café closed its doors in 1965 and was relocated to Albion Street, where it survived until the early 1970s. Despite the care taken to preserve the exterior of many buildings in Leeds, the painting of this one – possibly done in a refurbishment in 1989 – seems heavy-handed and inappropriate. Much of the detail seen on neighbouring properties is obscured. Officially Nos. 65–68 Briggate, it has had a chequered record for tenants in recent years, with Dixons, Currys, Republic (a jeans business founded in Leeds) and USC all coming and going before Lloyds Bank took up residence in 2016. Tenants between the 1960s and 1980s included Wakefield Army & Navy Stores, Millets, Timothy Whites chemists, Hepworth and Next. To the left, the large building occupying No. 64 Briggate and 13–14 Albion Street, Body Shop, has been Grade II listed since 1996. Some of the mythical creatures decorating the exterior are slightly worn, probably due to aggressive cleaning over the years.

# QUEEN'S ARCADE FROM BRIGGATE

This varied stretch of the main shopping street has hardly been altered since 1909

c. 1900

LEFT: In 1207, a street running from the River Aire north to Kirkgate was laid out by Maurice de Gant, the lord of the manor in Leeds. Literally the gateway to the bridge, it became known as Briggate. The modern layout was settled upon in 1626. Seen here around the turn of the twentieth century, a Thomas Potts clock marks the eastern end of Queen's Arcade, opened in 1889. Some residents referred to it as Fosters Arcade as the Fosters drapery and furnishings shop had been trading here since before the arcade was built. Dominating the skyline (and seen in images of this stretch of Briggate well into the 1960s) is No. 78, the home of Hope Brothers, a national menswear chain who were, 'hosiers, glovers and outfitters to all parts of the world'. The painted sign on the other side of the tower also listed them as tailors and hatters.

BELOW: More than a hundred years later, Queen's Arcade is still here, albeit with a different frontage flanked by different shops. Two buildings north, Thornton's Arcade is unmistakeable with its pointed-roof tower. The old Lockharts building between them at Nos. 76–77 was superseded in 1909 and given an Art Deco design on the front. No. 76 was an early branch of Marks & Spencer. The three-storey property at 85–87 Briggate, at the end of the parade, is a modern monstrosity. Currently occupied by Tesco Metro, it formerly housed the Lime fashion store and earlier a branch of Dorothy Perkins with Burton. The solid 1930s block of the former Lewis's store is a reminder of past retail glories, while the canopy on the right indicates the entrance to the Victoria Quarter, a modern success retail story. Note the entrance on the left, between EE and optician Ollie Quinn, to a ginnel leading to The Ship, one of Leeds' historic city centre pubs.

## BRIGGATE NORTH OF COUNTY ARCADE

Contrasting with the parade opposite, this stretch on the east side of Briggate has seen recent rebuilding

LEFT: One of the distinctive features of the city is the amazing variety of styles that were employed by the busy architects and builders. In this short parade on the eastern side of Briggate, taken on a sunny day in February 1944, we just see the boldly decorated exterior of County Arcade, faced in Burmantofts faience. The frontage of Dixons the furrier, at No. 98, cannot be said to blend in well with the 1898 original. A narrow ginnel leads to Bay Horse Hotel yard before we get to the compact branch of Stylo, the national footwear chain owned by the Ziff family of Leeds. Then there is a jump in size to Nos. 94–96 which house the Cash Boot Company and the Cash Clothing Co., 'The Peoples Clothiers'. The signs covering the upper floors made this one hard to miss even in Leeds' crowded city centre. (There had been a branch of the footwear business in Call Lane previously.)

ABOVE: The Art Nouveau-inspired black and gold name boards used across the Victoria Quarter may look a little twee or contrived to some eyes, but at least they are more sympathetic to their setting than Dixons' brash script of 1944. A furrier might now fit in with the luxury brand names that the Victoria Quarter has attracted, best represented by Louis Vuitton, which opened here in September 2006. To the left, the modern glass-fronted building occupied by Danish jeweller Pandora, designed by Campbell Associates, dates from 2010. Yorkshire Bank moved into the refurbished Nos. 94–96 in 2015. On the far left, at Nos. 92–93, is the Grade II-listed building that was the base of jeweller William Greenwood between 1920 and 1940. Tenants in these now-prime units had included Poundland, Borders Books and, back in the late 1990s, an independent gift shop called Spunky Monkey. How things have changed. Another sign of the changing times are the anti ram-raid barriers positioned outside Louis Vuitton, which was hit twice by thieves in April 2017.

c. 1900

# 110-111 BRIGGATE / HARVEY NICHOLS

Two premium fashion retailers occupied the same site, about 100 years apart

LEFT: Taken around 1900, this fine photograph is a reminder of the high standards achieved in window dressing long before it was called visual merchandising. It is also a celebration of the specialist retailer who deals, in depth, in only one category. John Taylor, hatter, at 110–11 Briggate, appears to be a Leeds-based business. The city's coat of arms is incorporated on the windows of both the ground and first floors and the sign above the door reveals that he had relocated here from 123 Kirkgate. Having been established in 1832, the business may have been forced to move by the building of the markets in Kirkgate in 1857, 1875 or 1904. The entire frontage is an explosion of different typefaces, slogans and signs (reportedly produced by Farrar Signs of Leeds). As well as sorting out new headgear from the vast selection within, customers could also tidy up hair and whiskers at the Empire Hairdressing Saloon and the Empire Shaving Saloon.

RIGHT: John Taylor's shop was immediately to the right of the Empire Theatre, one of Leeds' most popular entertainment venues. Part of the famous Moss Empire chain run by H. E. Moss, it opened on August 29th, 1898, as part of the new arcades complex. The arcades' architect Frank Matcham was best-known for designing theatres. The Empire seated more than 1,700 and boasted of modern wonders such as electric light and a fireproof curtain. It welcomed most of the big stars of the century, such as Laurel & Hardy. It was remodelled in 1931 to show films too and it lasted longer than many variety theatres, but its small stage was not suitable for the larger productions of the post-war world. The curtain finally came down on February 25th, 1961. The theatre was demolished and replaced with the Empire Arcade, which was opened in 1964. The arcade was superseded by Harvey Nichols, which opened on the site in 1996. All that's left of the Empire Theatre is a decorative plaque above the rear entrance to the premium department store in Cross Arcade.

c. 1905

# LEEDS PARISH CHURCH

Known for centuries as St Peter's, it is now officially styled Leeds Minster

ABOVE: On the site of several places of worship dating back to the eighth century, St Peter's was going to be improved in the late 1830s by Dean Walter Farquhar Hook, vicar of Leeds. Most of the existing medieval building was in such poor repair, however, that only the relatively recent south wall could be retained. The work cost £30,000 and the new parish church was consecrated on September 2nd, 1842. Designed by Robert Cantrell, St Peter's was supposedly the largest English church built since St Paul's Cathedral from 1675 to 1711. Additionally, it was the first major Anglican 'town church' that was meant to appeal to the rapidly disillusioned working classes. St Peter's was well-placed to minister to the needy as it was close to Quarry Hill, the most notorious of Leeds' many slums. In the church, Dean Hook, who died in 1875, has a memorial designed by George Gilbert Scott in the manner of a medieval shrine. It was sculpted by William Day Keyworth, who also created the four lions outside Leeds Town Hall.

ABOVE: The church has been Grade I listed since 1963. Its impressive interior can seat more than 1,600, but its regular congregation numbers only a few dozen. It missed out on becoming a cathedral, so since 2012 it has been Leeds Minster, officially the minster and parish church of St Peter-at-Leeds. The church, still with a working clock by Potts of Leeds in its tower, is open daily. Its attractions include The Leeds Cross, which was constructed using tenth-century pieces found during the rebuilding of 1838–42. It is a poignant connection with church and city origins. Since the first image was taken, we have lost St Peter's infants school, seen on the left. With an entrance on The Calls, the school was established in 1813 to educate poor children. It was demolished in the 1980s and its site is now occupied by Chantrell Court and Chantrell House, residential and office blocks.

# BARSTOW MANSION

This once-fashionable district was isolated from the city centre by the railway viaduct in the late 1860s

1906

LEFT: The area around St Peter's parish church had been fashionable for prosperous city burghers in the seventeenth century. Opposite the western entrance of the church, wealthy merchant Jeremiah Barstow had built his impressive mansion, but by 1906 the district had severely declined. By then the once-affluent residence was divided up and was, in part, Noble's Ideal Working Men's Home, a dormitory for labourers and other lower workers. The term 'Ideal' usually indicated that an establishment permitted no alcohol. Several broken window panes on the upper floors add to the depressing atmosphere. This photograph was taken in about 1906 by Leeds photographer Alf Mattison, just a year or two before the building was demolished. Among the many advertisements, some brands that survived until the modern era can be seen, such as Cadbury's Chocolate, Dewar's whisky, Player's Cigarettes and Brooke Bonds (sic) Tea.

BELOW: The railway line linking the North Eastern Railway with the Midland line at Leeds, constructed during 1864–69, became a boundary between the bustling city centre and the previously significant districts at the south-east end of Kirkgate. The parish church was on the outside of this new frontier in an area known by 1900 for its squalid yards, seedy inns and run-down lodging houses, like the old Barstow Mansion. The most decrepit buildings began to be cleared. The railway viaduct cut through St Peter's 'new burying ground', which had been in use since the 1830s. An act of parliament insisted the displaced headstones were laid out in the correct positions above the graves on the viaduct embankment, as seen in today's Penny Pocket Park, across the road from the church. The arches under the viaduct were once dark, unpleasant places, but like much of the area near the Aire waterfront, they have been improved in the past twenty-five or so years.

c. 1902

# THE VIEW FROM CROWN POINT BRIDGE

Desirable apartments stand on the site of the old tram electricity power station and a textile dyeworks

LEFT: Seen from Crown Point Bridge, the most easterly of the city crossings of the Aire, a new boiler house is being built for the Leeds Tramways Electricity Generating Station, opened in 1897 to provide power for the tram system. This image dates from about 1902 when expansion of the site continued as the demand for power increased. The boiler house was built on the site of the former premises of a maltster called George Ikin. The large chimney was part of Bowman Lane Dyeworks, founded in the late 1700s, which was one of Leeds' largest dye houses. Crown Point Bridge was built between 1840 and 1842 as a toll road linking Hunslet with east Leeds. Designed by George Leather, the iron casting work was handled by Park Ironworks in Sheffield. It cost £8,750 to build. It was named after Crown Point Wharf to the west, part of the Aire & Calder Navigation. Tolls were ended in 1868.

ABOVE: When Leeds City Council devised a plan of action to revitalise the run-down waterfront from the mid-1980s, a crucial element was the provision of a public riverside walkway. It starts here, in a development known as The Chandlers, which was opened in 1986. Designed by architects Denison Peters, it comprises eight blocks of flats, most newly built, but some converted from the former Turtons Crown Point Provender Mills of 1876. (William Turton was a corn and hay merchant, who from 1866 operated horse-drawn trams in Leeds.) Just beyond The Chandlers, the next block is called Langton's Wharf. Access to all the blocks is from The Calls, the name of which is believed to derive either from the Latin *callis*, meaning a narrow track, or from the wooden piles or 'calls' used to prevent the riverbank from being washed away. Even in modern Leeds, tangible and fascinating links to history are never very far away.

c. 1910

# LOOKING EASTWARDS FROM LEEDS BRIDGE

The remarkable refurbishment of the Leeds waterfront marked a new phase of commercial prosperity for the city

ABOVE: Contrary to the famous declaration found in Matthew 6:24, this image suggests Leeds found it possible to serve both God and Mammon. Probably taken in 1910 looking eastwards downstream from Leeds Bridge, the photograph shows part of the Aire & Calder Navigation's basin that was created in 1821. Nearest the camera on the left is Navigation Warehouse, later known as the British Waterways Warehouse.

The builders' merchant Atkinson, which had its entrance on The Calls, is dwarfed by the 7-storey Sparrows Wharf. The black spire of St Peter's parish church is seen in the centre. Just to the right of the church, on the bend in the river, is the triple-gabled Fletland Mills. At the right foreground are the warehouses on the Aire & Calder Navigation wharf.

136

ABOVE: It is difficult to imagine that by the 1970s the Leeds waterfront was virtually a no-go area for respectable citizens, a run-down district notorious for prostitution and crime. By the mid 1980s, the city council instigated a plan of action for the riverside, with the dramatic results that contributed to Leeds' resurgence. Symbolic of the transformation was the creation of the award-winning hotel, 42 The Calls, in the former Fletland Mills building. The smart Calls Landing building stands next to it. Sparrow Wharf was converted into Halsbury House, a mixture of office and residential units. Navigation Warehouse became Riverside Court, a two-block development of about forty-six residential units built around a courtyard. On the south bank, the pale-coloured apartment block is Dock House. The smaller brick building is Flax House. Both are part of the Victoria Quays area that was officially opened in September 1987. On the north bank a gap remains undeveloped, but a hoarding round the site promises 'a new vibrant waterside destination' is 'coming soon'.

1973

# LEEDS BRIDGE VIEWED FROM THE EAST

The original settlement of Leeds is presumed to have been very near this crossing

LEFT: Medieval Leeds developed on the north bank of the Aire. From 1207 Briggate, literally the bridge gate, ran north from here to Woodhouse Moor. A stone bridge, now known as Old Leeds Bridge, stood here from about 1376. It was enlarged several times before being demolished in 1869. The Leeds Bridge seen here was constructed in 1870—73 by Thomas Dyne Steel using wrought- and cast-iron manufactured by John Butler of Stanningley. It cost over £50,000. Viewed from the north bank looking west in 1973, the white building on the southern end of the bridge was the premises of ironmonger Hicks Bros. From a second-floor window in 1888, Louis Le Prince filmed the scene on Leeds Bridge, which is generally regarded to be the world's first motion picture, although some people argue that he made his first film in a garden in Roundhay. The modern building in the centre was the canteen at the Leeds City Transport bus depot on Swinegate.

ABOVE: The Leeds Civic Trust's Blue Plaque on the riverside wall records the opening of the Aire & Calder Navigation in 1700, which enabled cloth produced in Leeds to be exported via Hull. The old wharves and warehouses have been converted into mainly residential blocks on this stretch or replaced by buildings that echo their Georgian and Victorian originals. On the north side, we see Riverside Court on this side of the bridge, with Windsor House, The Studios and The Quays running westwards beyond the bridge. On the south side, in an area known since 1987 as Victoria Quays, Calder House is nearest the camera, with Dock House and Aire House between it and the bridge. Beyond the crossing is the area known as Bridge End, which has been left behind somewhat in Leeds' urban renaissance, but there are indications that the patches of derelict land and neglected buildings will soon be upgraded like their neighbours.

1903

# GRANARY WHARF

The largest area of redevelopment of the Leeds waterfront happened here, right behind City Station

LEFT: Leeds is a long way from the sea, but by 1700, with finance from Leeds and Wakefield merchants, it was an inland port thanks to the Aire & Calder Navigation that stretched eastwards to link the city with Hull. To connect with the transatlantic trade from the west coast, in 1777 the first part of the 127-mile Leeds and Liverpool canal was opened. By 1816 it reached Liverpool and so Leeds stood on a waterway that stretched from the Mersey to the Humber. In this 1903 photo, looking westwards from Victoria Bridge over the Aire, the start of the Leeds and Liverpool canal, known as the River Lock, can be seen to the left. The canal here was built on the course of the Hol Beck, the stream that gave the district its name. River Lock had an unusually deep, 11 foot 3 inch lift to accommodate coal barges, such as those seen in the right foreground alongside the Leeds Industrial Cooperative Society Coal Wharf. The cranes were probably made locally by Booths of Rodley.

ABOVE: The redevelopment of the Leeds waterfront since the late 1980s has been remarkable, transforming near derelict industrial units into attractive contemporary offices, residential blocks and leisure units, as well as making the river an attraction in itself. This panorama of Granary Wharf, behind Leeds City Station, is particularly impressive. From the left we see Granary Building (formerly New Centaur House), the base of menswear group BMB. In the distance is the 2 Whitehall Riverside office block, just off Whitehall Road. The circular tower is Candle House, an apartment block finished in 2009. The red brick building in the centre, the 13-storey Doubletree Hilton Hotel, was opened in 2014, five years after the large mixed-use Waterman's Place block to the right. At the edge of the image is the Direct Line insurance office, which has its main entrance on Neville Street. Just to the south of Victoria Bridge, out of shot, is Bridgewater Place. Completed in 2007, at 367 feet high, this office and residential block of 32 storeys is the tallest building in Yorkshire.

c. 1935

# TEMPLE WORKS

One of the country's most extraordinary industrial buildings is in peril

ABOVE: The son of a Briggate linen draper, John Marshall was one of the first millionaires of the Industrial Revolution and MP for Yorkshire between 1826 and 1830. He is best remembered today, however, for Temple Works, this extraordinary industrial building in Marshall Street, Holbeck, just to the south-west of City Square. Designed for him by architect Joseph Bonomi in 1838–40 as a flax mill, its facade was inspired by the Temple of Antaeopolis in Tjebu and the Temple of Horus at Edfu, both in Egypt; the link being that flax, the raw fibre from which linen is woven, was widely used in ancient Egypt. The Temple Works frontage, built from coarse gritstone, led to a vast weaving shed covering 2 acres, which was thought at the time to be the largest single room in the world. To the right of this site, Marshall had set up a 4-storey flax mill in 1791–92, drawing water from the Hol Beck to power his machinery. After a fire, that was replaced between 1815 and 1831 by a 6-storey building – Marshall's Mill – that still stands.

ABOVE: Grade I listed since 1951, Temple Works (also called Temple Mills) has been on Historic England's At Risk register for many years, the victim of decay and neglect. This often-photographed 2-storey building is only the office block of the 2-acre site. The main building's frontage stretches away for more than 140 yards, displaying another eighteen columns to complement the six seen here. Scaffolding now holds it up. Marshall's celebrated flax mill ceased to operate as long ago as 1886. Subsequent tenants have included clothing manufacturer James Rhodes and Co. around 1900, Samuel Driver, and the mail order company Kay & Co. In recent years, part of the building was used as an arts centre. In January 2018, developer CEG (formerly Commercial Estates Management) bought Temple Works for just £1 with the intention of repairing and redeveloping it. As this book went to press, Leeds City Council was working with CEG on the project as part of its wider regeneration of the South Bank of the Aire. (NB This is not Marshall's Mill – that is a different building just to the west of Temple Works.)

# INDEX